SHELL

SHELL

A Completely Untrue, Totally Made-Up
Tale About Not Working at a Startup

A Novel

Bree Steele

NEW DEGREE PRESS

SHELL

A Completely Untrue, Totally Made-Up Tale

About Not Working at a Startup

ISBN

978-1-63676-709-3 *Paperback*

978-1-63730-058-9 *Kindle Ebook*

978-1-63730-160-9 *Digital Ebook*

To all my coworkers, past, present, and future—but mostly the sane ones.

CONTENTS

AUTHOR'S NOTE

Now, more than ever, we live in an age of misinformation. Surrounded by an endless stream of data. An incomprehensible amount of content. Instantaneous answers. With over personalization and infinite scrolling, a handful of technology companies control most of what we see. Discerning fact from fiction is challenging.

Over the past few years, we have witnessed some of the dangers of relying too much on Big Tech. Filter bubbles. Echo chambers. Fake news. All contribute to an overwhelming feeling of fatigue.

So what happens when the rules and predictability of traditional workplaces are stripped away? Enter the World of Startups. Meet the New Hire and her numerous colleagues: the Chief Happiness Officer, the Tech Czar, the Vice President of Marketing, the Stepdaughter, and the Founder. A hot, up-and-coming business filled with big dreams and even bigger personalities. Perhaps, maybe a secret or two. Welcome to the New Frontier, where nothing is what it seems, and it's hard to tell friend from foe. The experiences of the New Hire reflect the uncertain times in which we live.

Having worked in Big Tech for many years, I always thought it would be interesting to reveal a little bit of what really goes on behind-the-scenes. Set in this fast-paced and constantly changing environment, the rules do not apply.

But what if something goes wrong? Without the usual guideposts, do we lose our way? Would we even know if we did?

While I never made the leap to Startupland, I certainly know about large corporations run by the cult of personalities. I understand how easy it is to become entrenched within a company's culture. We want to believe, so we do—especially when the leader is charismatic. Self-preservation is a much stronger motivator than people think. And it is much easier to get stuck in a trap than getting out of one. This make-believe world is the fertile ground for our story.

My intent for this book is to give readers a better understanding of the digital workplace and a chance to explore the untamed wilds of this Brave New World. I paint an atmosphere so ambiguous that gray becomes the dominant color. As with any good story, the evidence is all there, perhaps right under our nose, but the trick, of course, is knowing where to look.

CHAPTER 1

I CAN'T TELL YOU WHY

London 2016. After ten years and two continents, this time the Search Engine was really falling apart. The New Hire's tenure was coming to an end. She finally had become a British citizen, her singular goal for seven consecutive years. She had gained all the rights and privileges afforded to members of the European Union. Then Brexit.

Business in the region was in decline. It had been for years. The New Hire had grown restless in London. Life was stuck on repeat. She loved the travel and the freedom, but was there something more? She grew tired of dark mornings and even darker afternoons. She longed for temperatures above sixty-eight degrees Fahrenheit. Maybe it was time for her to move back to California.

With the tedium of her job beginning to cement, the New Hire felt trapped. Negotiating team goals. Justifying headcount. Answering the same fundamental questions day after day. Whenever she was

stuck in a conference room explaining yet again how the platform's algorithm worked, right on cue, the sun would make an appearance. Its strong rays would blind the New Hire momentarily before dissolving seemingly forever into the overcast sky. Was the universe telling her something?

The New Hire started to imagine herself back in Los Angeles, enjoying uncloudy days filled with endless sunshine. The rise of nationalism in Europe added to her growing discontent. She questioned everything.

The Search Engine made all its money in the States. Europe could barely cover the electricity bill with the revenue they contributed to the bottom line. As a result, the New Hire was forced to lay off half her staff due to "strategic decisions" (read: cost exceeded profit). Suddenly, everything felt real. This was not the usual panic-and-swirl that distracted employees' thoughts and attentions without any lasting damage. This was tangible. Consequential. Human lives were being affected by these directives.

Other expatriates had told her she would know when it was time to go home. Without realizing it, the New Hire's stint away from the States had changed her. Not so much in tectonic movements, but in smaller, more rotational ways. She felt out of place. Caught between two worlds. Was this her pink moment—that period when the setting sun illuminates nature's surroundings perfectly, when everything becomes clear? The New Hire convinced herself there would be a sign, but maybe not.

As she neared the end of her time at the Search Engine, she would often hear the familiar verses of Peggy Lee's most famous song swirling around in her head. When the New Hire gently closed her eyes, she could not help but mouth the same conclusion, “Is That All There Is?”

* * *

Los Angeles 2016. Renewed hope. A fresh start. A clean slate. The New Hire left the Search Engine and the UK, excited to explore opportunities in California, her home for many years before her detour in Europe. She was not in a rush to find her next big job. She wanted the right fit. Change. She focused her attention on startups. Cutting-edge ideas. Entrepreneurial-minded people. An opportunity to leave Corporate America and try something different. Then Donald Trump.

The New Hire felt an underlying sense of anxiety. She left England as uncertainty and greater geopolitical forces were gathering. The brewing storm would soon consume people’s lives. Moving back, did she just trade one tumultuous situation for another?

When the Chief Happiness Officer called her for an interview, the New Hire was excited. The company and the job description checked all the right boxes. Developing a mobile app from scratch. Owning the strategy. Working collaboratively. Not saving lives, but the business had a do-good slant.

The New Hire felt she had a chance to make a difference. Early phase. Projected to become a significant player. A disruptive force. Everything felt enticing.

COMPANY DESCRIPTION

We are an early phase startup located in Hollywood, California. We are an exciting new venture destined to become a significant and immediate player in the app universe. Come join us today. We will be a major disruptive force in the marketplace!

We value diversity, working collaboratively as a team, and fostering synergies between our team's interests, skills, and strengths. We are dedicated to growing our business. We are passionate about creating a unique mobile app with a unique immersive experience.

SUMMARY OF POSITION

The Senior Strategy Director will run strategic initiatives, grow client programs, drive business development, and provide strong cross-functional collaboration.

ESSENTIAL DUTIES

- Manage the overall vision and strategy
- Develop requirements necessary to fuel user growth and product evolution
- Own the product roadmap, recommending and leading priorities
- Understand what features drive and impact revenue
- Define success metrics and analyze performance
- Weigh trade-offs between user engagement, feature benefits, and cost
- Build strong, collaborative relationships across departments
- Lead cross-functional teams in delivering a quality product
- Be the expert in operations

The New Hire had never spent much time in Hollywood, only visiting the familiar tourist destinations—the Walk of Fame, the Chinese Theater, the Hollywood Bowl. Beyond the glamour and glitz of the large boulevards was another part of the city. Hidden in plain sight but still somehow forgotten.

Called Historic Hollywood on several mobile phone map applications, several big brands and fast-growing startups had discovered this district as prime real estate for creative office space. New builds were in progress next to dilapidated apartments and long-vacant storefronts. Food carts pushing fresh fruit with spicy toppings occasionally appeared while trendy, organic eateries monopolized many of the available leases.

Arriving early for her interview, the New Hire parked her car and walked around the block to gather her thoughts. Once notable, the neighborhood felt mostly left behind. Surrounded by narrow alleys and uneven sidewalks, the Startup was close to a long-promised metro line. Across the way sat a dusty, abandoned lot. The streets were metaphors for the city itself.

The disparity between the rich and the poor was apparent. Men and women in dark blue suits crossed busy intersections. They walked hurriedly, trying not to notice the downtrodden littering the walkways. The double-decker buses filled with international visitors skipped this area.

Mentally prepared, the New Hire approached the entrance. Occupying a full city block, the building's previous tenant was a large, well-known department store. Setting up shop in this formerly grand high-rise made sense for an up-and-coming startup.

The once magnificent building offered a heavy nod to the city's Art Deco past. An anachronistic symbol of its old glory—majestic eagle heads, intricate artisan designs, beautifully aged marble accents. Endless promise, but unrealized potential. The perfect place to gather a group of willing underdogs desperate to get their hands dirty and improve the world.

The entire setting was slightly past its prime but ready for a comeback—the perpetual lottery player whose luck could change at any moment. The building reflected how the New Hire felt.

"Yes, I have your name here," the well-dressed man at the security desk said. "If you can please show me your driver's license, I will create a temporary ID for you."

Waiting for the pass to print, the New Hire thought how seamless the process was. All terribly official, important even.

"We're all set. If you will, I am happy to escort you." The security guard led the New Hire through a glass barrier to an open elevator door. With his badge, he selected the number seven from the control panel. "On your way out, please drop your pass back at the front desk. Have a nice day."

The Mobile App Startup's space was a short walk from the elevator bank, taking up most of the seventh floor. The Chief Happiness Officer greeted the New Hire at the glass doors.

"Sorry for the mess. We are in the process of upgrading. This is our visitor entrance. I'll take you through to meet our Chief Information Officer and Vice President of Marketing. They'll be conducting the interview today."

The New Hire took in her surroundings. She observed a well-worn, olive-colored velvet couch and a small group of desks. The furniture was simple, bought in bulk from a large Swedish manufacturer. Extremely neo-tech.

"Did you have any trouble getting here?"

"No, it was very easy. Thank you for asking."

"Before I forget, if you want to give me your parking ticket, I can validate it for you."

The Chief Happiness Officer walked over to the large wooden desk, which sat in the middle of the oversized room. Opening the drawer, she pulled out a stamp.

"Here you go. Shall we meet the others?"

"Sounds great."

"I'll tell you this section of the office once housed the dining and banquet hall for department store staff. There's also a theater and some wardrobe rooms in the back. The layout will make more sense when we get to the main area. Also, we own the sixth and eighth floors, so we are planning to grow in the near future. Currently, we are remodeling downstairs for an eventual move."

Turning the corner, the New Hire saw several long tables lining the impressive open plan. The space was bright, lit by floor-to-ceiling windows, and further accented with a grandiose balcony offering decent city views.

Like the iconic building, however, the office needed some work around the edges. Gilded on the outside, crumbling on the inside. If you looked closely, the foundation for greatness was there.

Art Deco motifs were plentiful. Geometric lines. Distinctive patterns. Stainless steel. The commitment to the century-old architecture movement was omnipresent. It enhanced the imperative nature of the Startup's mission: disrupt the marketplace and become a major player in the app universe.

The Chief Happiness Officer and the New Hire passed a small kitchen that likely was once a wait-station in its previous incarnation. The space was complete with two sinks, a full-sized refrigerator, and a large cutout where staff once placed freshly made drinks. From there, massive doors opened into a theater, which was no longer actively used. A podium, complete with audio equipment and surround sound, stood in the middle of the stage. It was hard not to see the potential. The New Hire could envision herself at a companywide meeting announcing the Startup was going public.

After walking through the theater, the two arrived in a backstage area that housed long-out-of-use dressing rooms for performers. In its prime, guests would have been thoroughly impressed by the journey that led to this spot. Considering the vastness of the office, though, interviewing candidates in this deeply secluded location seemed like an odd choice.

The Chief Happiness Officer opened the door to the green wardrobe. It was a small space with no windows and bright, theatrical lights. It reminded the New Hire of Max Factor's World-Famous Makeup Rooms at the Hollywood Museum. Depending on the starlet's hair color, the cosmetic artist would choose the designated place for either Blondes, Redheads, Brownettes, or Brunettes. Painted a specifically selected monotone color, these rooms ensured the young ingenue always looked her best and that Max could apply his Color Harmony techniques.

The pale beige walls combined with the hot-red spotlights in the green wardrobe room, however, did no favors for the New Hire. Perhaps once perfect for putting on makeup, the lighting was not so great for impressing strangers during an interview.

Upon entering the room, a friendly voice announced herself through the almost blinding glare: "Welcome. I'm the Vice President of Marketing. I own the company branding. I run Sales and Marketing and oversee Design." The woman was attractive, confident, and effortlessly fashionable. She spoke with kindness.

The New Hire felt at ease until a second voice said: "And I'm the Chief Information Officer, also known as the Tech Czar. I'm responsible for all the Startup's technological needs."

The second woman offered a firm handshake and seemed to be pumping out her chest. The New Hire immediately noticed her creaseless button-down shirt tucked in far too low. The Tech Czar wore her hair in what appeared to be a painfully tight ponytail. It reminded the New Hire of Muscles, Jerry's overly fit cousin from the old cat-and-mouse cartoons.

Trying to continue with an open mind, the New Hire sat down. She placed her shoulder bag by her feet and pulled out a notebook and pen. Expecting some small talk, she was ready to discuss the weather, traffic, or the stately building.

Without missing much of a beat, the Tech Czar continued midsentence talking to the VP. "I told my wife she had to pick up the kid. She's insisting on dance lessons after school. That's fine by me, but I'm not driving crosstown during rush hour to drop the kid off for an hour lesson. What am I supposed to do in that hour? Wait for her in the parking lot?"

The New Hire offered a sympathetic glance but felt like she was interrupting a not particularly interesting story. The Tech Czar's unusually prominent belt buckle caught her eye. For a slight woman, the oversized initials from a famous designer appeared out of place. The Tech Czar's demeanor was a stark contrast to the instant warmth emanating from the VP, who tried to make the New Hire feel comfortable.

Transitioning from the tales of childcare woes, the VP looked at the New Hire and asked, "How was it getting to the office? Did you hit a lot of traffic?"

"Very easy. I only live a few miles away, so the commute was painless." The New Hire was careful to come across as fully engaged, even when discussing innocuous topics.

As she studied her potential employers, she thought something was off with the Tech Czar. This wasn't just your quirky, work-in-tech oddness, but something else. Something palpable. An almost innate awkwardness around other human beings.

Since the New Hire was interviewing for a strategy role, she expected and carefully prepared for questions like: "What was your thinking behind that?" or "Why did you make that decision?" The standard fare of can-you-do-this-job inquiries. Conversation starters to get a dialogue going. Perhaps, a few softballs to develop a rhythm. Something to gain more insight as to why someone might be a good fit in a creative, fast-paced environment.

Instead, the Tech Czar preferred to have side conversations with the VP, whom she frequently referred to as Pookie.

"Pookie, do we have an art meeting this afternoon? What did Design say about the wireframes?" the Tech Czar inquired.

"You know Design. They always have something to say. And yes, I think the meeting is this afternoon," the VP responded.

"Fine. Let's go to Grand Central Market for lunch."

Strange, yes, but alarm bells were not quite ringing yet for the New Hire. She understood that in the world of startups, one must deal with a fair number of eccentric personalities who compensate for whatever they lack in social skills with their technical know-how, deep backend understanding, and programming ability.

However, it was hard for the New Hire not to think the Tech Czar was conducting an interview with someone else. At several points, the New Hire stopped herself from looking around and asking, "Are you talking to me?"

The New Hire reminded herself that this is what she wanted. She wanted to join a startup. She wanted to build a product from scratch.

Whenever someone spoke, the Tech Czar moved her glance in the general direction from where the sounds were emanating but never quite made eye contact. At one point, the Tech Czar appeared to be staring at the New Hire as if she had a spot on her shirt. In self-doubt, the New Hire nonchalantly glanced down, thinking she might have missed a button. Eventually, she realized the Tech Czar was simply looking in her general vicinity instead of directly at her.

The New Hire continually refocused the interview by highlighting her strengths. She tried to stay on topic and meet her objectives; show why she was the right person for this role.

Luckily, the Tech Czar was happy enough to let the VP ask most of the questions. Despite the unusual nature of the format, the meeting went well. The New Hire had a good feeling from the VP. During the discussion, the pair swapped stories about living and working abroad.

"I grew up here in Los Angeles. My family has been here for generations. I moved to Paris after college, but I felt pulled back to the States after ten years."

Like the New Hire, the VP had worked at other large, matrixed organizations. When the VP mentioned she previously worked at a global multilevel marketing company, the one that had sold herbal dietary supplements, it did give the New Hire a slight pause.

"Yeah, I worked there for seventeen years. Can you believe it?" the VP said.

Deciding *everyone has to work somewhere*, the New Hire chose not to fixate on the idea of spending almost two decades at an organization that was likely a pyramid scheme.

After an hour, the interview came to a natural stopping point. The VP volunteered to walk the New Hire out. They engaged in effortless small talk as they headed toward the elevator.

"I definitely miss living overseas," the VP confided.

"Yes, it was an exceedingly difficult decision to come back to the US. As they say, 'Tired of London, tired of life.'"

"I bet."

The VP reassured the New Hire that the Startup would be in touch shortly. "You can expect to hear from us within a day or so. We move quickly here! If you have any additional questions, please let me know," she offered, pulling out a business card.

When the elevator doors closed, the New Hire felt genuine enthusiasm. While she was not 100 percent sold on the Tech Czar, she liked the VP. From what she understood about the role, the job itself was appealing. Building a new product. Owning the strategy. Room to grow. An opportunity to do something different.

Within twenty-four hours, the Chief Happiness Officer called. "The team was extremely impressed with you and your expertise. We are very close to making our final selection, and you are our top candidate. Would you be open to a follow-up call? Our Tech Czar has some additional questions."

Of course she does.

The Chief Happiness Officer arranged a phone interview for another round of queries. While the New Hire felt confident, she was also slightly nervous. The Tech Czar barely spoke during the initial interview. The questions she did ask were difficult for the New Hire to follow. *What exactly did she want to clarify?*

Having no idea what to expect in a second conversation, the New Hire went back to the familiar—studying. She pored over her notes from their first meeting. Since the New Hire could not imagine what the Tech Czar was trying to gain from the initial interview, she was unsure where she should focus her attention for round two.

In her initial jottings, the New Hire wrote ADA with a question mark. She vaguely recalled discussion about website compliance, but it seemed like a weird question to ask a strategy person. Having deflected the topic in the first conversation, the New Hire tried consuming everything she could on the subject through research. Her real plan, however, was to try to distract the Tech Czar by asking personal questions. She knew people loved to talk about themselves. If the New Hire could casually redirect the Tech Czar down a rabbit hole, she might be okay.

* * *

The phone rang at the set time. The Tech Czar immediately began: "Okay. You're from the South, right? So, which football team?"

Oh god, a sports question.

This was the category in Trivial Pursuit the New Hire always avoided. She could be stuck for hours trying to get the orange wedge. And football? Was she supposed to say a southern team? Did she even know the name of any southern teams?

As the New Hire searched her memory for a coherent answer, she smiled to herself. *What did she expect? Could there be a more perfect, completely irrelevant, off-the-wall non sequitur question?* An offbeat question from an offbeat person.

Taking a moment before answering, the New Hire tried to recall anything she could about football teams or players. She remembered once hearing Joe Namath on *The Howard Stern Show.* Broadway Joe. The larger-than-life personality. The fur coats. The surprise Super Bowl win. Now stuck in her head, the New Hire blurted out: "The Jets."

Continuing, she said, "I know. It's an unconventional choice. I'm not even from New York. But like all Jets fans, I really only watch the games to boo them. For us loyalists, they never fail to disappoint. Each year, sportscasters predict that this will be the year, but they never even make it to the playoffs." At least, that is what the New Hire had heard. She honestly had no idea.

Pleased by the unexpectedness of the answer, the Tech Czar continued to make several other unrelated inquiries. From the New Hire's perspective, the only common denominator was most questions had little to do with strategy.

The Tech Czar rapid-fired through several topics, barely waiting for a response: "What's your approach to app design architecture? How do you think about ensuring compliance? What are your thoughts on Agile?"

Not at all confident in what she was saying, the New Hire remained calm and answered as best she could. The Tech Czar did not seem to be listening anyway. After twenty minutes, the call ended.

The New Hire felt she had a fifty-fifty shot at the job. Even money.

Within a few hours, the Chief Happiness Officer phoned and offered her the position.

The New Hire had been exploring the possibility of working at a number of different startups. Convinced this new avenue would provide the change she sought, she weighed her options.

The Chief Happiness Officer said almost sixty people (some remote) filled the halls of the former department store's headquarters. A plus.

Another viable opportunity was from a company within walking distance from the New Hire's apartment. They made her a verbal offer. She had instantly connected with the married couple who ran the prospective startup and were the only employees. They gave her a bottle of Perrier and a hug at the end of the interview.

The New Hire ran through the pros and cons of the two prospects with a trusted friend. "Okay, but what happens when the husband and wife get mad at you?" her confidant asked. Two-against-one stuck in the back of the New Hire's head.

Confident most businesses populate their staffs with characters from the Island of Misfit Toys, the New Hire focused on each role's day-to-day responsibilities. One would be working with a lovely couple, managing content strategy. With the Mobile App Startup, she would be more hands-on. She could develop and launch a product. Make an impact. Build something. See it in a store. That was what excited her.

Leaving behind Corporate America had disadvantages. Okay, so this meant no more free lunches for the New Hire. Literally. At the Search Engine, she had grown accustomed to hot and cold choices every day. She would especially miss the breakfast bar: scrambled eggs, fresh avocado, the occasional chocolate or almond croissant. She loved the accouterments and prestige of the Search Engine, but it was time to move on.

Taking a job at a startup was what the New Hire wanted, right? The offer met all of her core requirements: unlimited vacation days, free health insurance, and a respectable salary. Sure, she would not have stock options or a 401K anymore, but that was on the roadmap.

After months of drifting since her return stateside, the New Hire could see safe shores. It was time to reenter work life and accept the consequences of making a decision. She felt that excitement and nervousness from embarking on something different. The next chapter. A new phase.

In her head, the New Hire knew change was necessary to grow, so she accepted the position, agreeing to start in three weeks. She took the time off to overanalyze her choice. She wanted to avoid the reality of her situation, even if only temporarily. She would be the New Kid in Town—again. Certainly, a familiar feeling, if not a comfortable one.

In high school, she had a friend who used to say: "Procrastination is the key." To what, the New Hire was never sure, but those words became her unofficial mantra. She found the best way to combat any indecisiveness was to run the clock out. A decision that did not seem like a decision because she had no other options. This was her modus operandi.

Processing and accepting the magnitude of her choice would wait until the night before her first day. Keen to maximize her final days of freedom, the New Hire booked a beach vacation on the Eastern Seaboard. She planned to arrive back in Los Angeles on the last flight out the Sunday before her Monday start date. At least, that was her plan.

CHAPTER 2

DARK SIDE OF THE MOON

For the New Hire, there was always something comforting about being at the airport. Something familiar. Something Zen. The comings and goings. The buzz. A world within a world. Endless possibilities. Regardless of flight length, it was a chance to be offline, unable to connect with the outside world, and unreachable. No distractions. Travel, her safe space.

Doubt, however, began seeping into her thinking, like the color from a teabag, slowly clouding lukewarm water. The strategy position would be an intellectual challenge, but the New Hire had spent her whole career working at big corporations. She had given a decade of her life to the Search Engine, habituated to its ways. Having staff, resources, and clout. She did think working at the Startup could be a great opportunity—until it was her turn to make the coffee.

The New Hire had traveled to the East Coast to relax. She wanted to enjoy what felt like the last days of summer before the next school year. Thirteen days before her official start date, the Chief Happiness Officer called.

"The Founder would like you to attend a two-day conference. I know and apologize because it's really short notice. Do you think you can get to Las Vegas by Wednesday night? The meetings are on Thursday and Friday."

The New Hire was not too keen to cut her trip short, but she didn't sense much of a choice. She heard herself blurt out: "Sure. I can make it happen. I'll need to move a few things around, but, yes, I'm sure I can find a way to arrive the day after tomorrow."

"Excellent! We really appreciate your flexibility. I'll email you the details shortly. Just keep track of all your expenses, and we'll reimburse you. There'll be a link to register for the conference, which you should do now. Please book your flights as soon as possible too. You can coordinate your hotel with the Tech Czar. She'll meet you there."

The Tech Czar! Three days together in Las Vegas? Alone? Together?

Since showing up in a bathing suit and flip-flops might not send the right message, the New Hire immediately hit a few local shops in the vacation town to prepare for the week ahead. Since she had planned to be on the East Coast for three weeks, the New Hire would keep her original flight back to Los Angeles and simply take a few days out of her holiday to attend the conference.

Problem number one: Buying clothes was not the New Hire's favorite activity. Buying clothes for an event with an ambiguous dress code and a strict deadline made it even less enjoyable. Finding clothes that belonged into the nebulous casual-but-appropriate category would have been challenging under any circumstance. Locating stores in a beach town with even a hint of corporate-lite attire—almost impossible.

After a quick map search, the New Hire found a large off-price retailer fourteen miles away. This was it. One-shot to buy everything. While the conference was only technically two days, she was arriving the night before. Although unlikely, the New Hire felt she ought to plan for the prospect of a dinner with the Tech Czar. She made a list: shoes, daywear (x3), and night out (x1).

The New Hire went through the store in record time. She made a quick scan of the layout and proceeded to pull anything that could possibly work. Maintaining it is always easier to edit, she grabbed a handful of options. Her motto: Beggars can't be choosers. The key was to find good enough, stat!

Problem number two: The Tech Czar also would be attending the conference. From their first and only in-person encounter, the New Hire felt unsure about how they would work together. Their past conversations did not have a natural flow. She worried about spending three days alone with the Tech Czar. *What would they talk about?*

Not many things bothered the New Hire, but she did not like uncomfortable silence. The Tech Czar was undeniably awkward, and this made the New Hire nervous.

Trying not to obsess over the days ahead, the New Hire packed her newly purchased clothes and mentally prepared for her unplanned prework adventure: three nights and two days in Las Vegas.

* * *

As the airplane made its slow descent into McCarran International, the New Hire thought about how different Las Vegas looked from the sky. The endless miles of city lights and urban sprawl hid the high desert in plain sight. Before long, she began to recognize the distinctive and instantly recognizable skyline of the Strip. Giant, imposing casino hotels placed just over the horizon.

The trance of the flight broke when the wheels touched down. The peaceful-easy feeling the New Hire had all but disappeared as quickly as the temporary winnings of an unsuspecting novice at the casino for the first time. The Tech Czar had told her to book the MGM Grand. While certainly not the most luxurious hotel on the Strip, it was definitely high-end for an up-and-coming Startup. It connected with a convention center, where the first meeting was to begin the following morning.

The New Hire did not know what to expect. At least, she thought, the accommodation would be nice. While she anxiously anticipated the two-day conference, most concerning was the idea of spending so much time with the Tech Czar.

After arriving, the New Hire waited a few hours to make contact. Of course, as a courtesy, she wanted to let the Tech Czar know she had arrived safely. Practically, however, she wanted to avoid any suggestion of a welcome drink together. The conference had an early start, so they agreed by text to meet in the lobby for breakfast.

Feeling a sense of relief, the New Hire reviewed the agenda for the conference. As was commonplace, concurrent talks were scheduled throughout the day. A choose-your-own-adventure for attendees.

With all the speaker events overlapping, she felt the best strategy was to divide and conquer. The session descriptions focused mostly on backend coding. The topics were interesting, if not all that relevant, particularly since the New Hire was employed to handle strategy.

Meeting in the lobby as agreed, the New Hire greeted the Tech Czar in a friendly tone.

"Hi! Nice to see you again. Thank you for including me. I'm looking forward to the next two days."

"Oh yeah. No problem."

"How was your trip in?"

"Fine."

The Tech Czar loved to talk in binary code, all zeros and ones. The New Hire had worked with similar people before. Typical conversations usually went something like:

"How was lunch?"

"Good."

"What did you order?"

"The special."

"What was the special?"

"A sandwich."

As frustrating as these monosyllabic answers could be, without fail, whenever asked to make a point-blank decision, these types of people would become uncontrollably chatty.

In their future interactions, the New Hire discovered these qualities to be especially reflective of the Tech Czar. Whenever asked a straightforward yes or no question, instead, she would explain why.

"Did you decide to get rid of the paid project-management software?" the New Hire would ask.

"Well, I can see it from both sides," the Tech Czar answered, hedging her response.

"Okay, so, is that a yes?"

"No, but I can see it from both sides."

"Okay, is that a no?"

"No. I mean, it is a yes and a no."

"Final answer?"

Struggling to gain any traction from the how-was-your-trip inquires, the New Hire redirected the Tech Czar's attention to the day that lay ahead.

"Shall we grab something to eat? Maybe we can review the agenda and see what looks worthwhile."

The pair walked silently toward the banquet hall. It was full of dozens of oversized circular tables, covered in overbleached, paper-thin, off-white linen. As they separated to prepare plates from the buffet, the New Hire felt like she was at one of those out-of-town weddings where you only know the bride and the groom. She was determined to build a connection with the Tech Czar, or at least try.

"You said the flight was uneventful. When did you arrive?"

"No issues. I arrived Monday."

"Nice, so you've had some time to settle in. Did you explore the casino? Or some of the shopping?"

"Yeah. A little of both."

"Fun. Did you win?"

"No."

"I guess that sounds about right."

At this point, the exchange was about what the New Hire expected. It was painfully clear the Tech Czar was going to stick with one-word answers. Realizing she needed to pull the ripcord on the small talk, the New Hire decided it was best to manage the situation proactively and set the direction.

Changing course, the New Hire focused on the conference. "Did you have a chance to review the agenda yet?"

"Yes. The talks look interesting."

"Shall we pick the sessions we most want to attend and then see if there is any overlap?"

"Sounds good."

As she was whisked away, at great expense, for only a few days to Las Vegas, the New Hire assumed the goal of the conference was for her and the Tech Czar to absorb as much content as humanly feasible in the shortest amount of time.

She carefully reread the topics, strategically selecting the most relevant sessions to her, but maybe also subconsciously, the ones least relevant to the Tech Czar.

* * *

The New Hire focused on taking diligent notes throughout the sessions. Her assessment: interesting enough, but where is the relevance? At one point, she pulled out her phone and reread the Startup's description of the job she had accepted. How could the content of this conference remotely relate to her day-to-day responsibilities?

The talks grew endless as the morning wore on, lasting anywhere from one to two hours. Approaching the lunch break, the New Hire became nervous about spending one-on-one time with the Tech Czar. She had little desire to sit in awkward, painful silence again.

Recapping her experiences so far, the New Hire had managed the first day of the trip successfully by arriving on the last flight into Las Vegas. Breakfast was fine because they planned out how they were going to cover the sessions. Now, lunch!

Maybe they could talk about what they had learned so far or introduce themselves to other strangers and make somewhat less uncomfortable small talk. Neither option was that appealing.

Unlike earlier in the day, where people could flow in and out of the breakfast room for either a sit-down meal or quick snack, a dedicated hour was set aside for all attendees to eat lunch. As the New Hire walked into the dining area, the Tech Czar motioned her to the spot she had picked out.

Super.

"Hey there. How are you enjoying the day so far?" the New Hire asked as she dropped her notebook on the table. She noticed the Tech Czar was already eating.

"Good."

"Good, good. I'm really enjoying the sessions too. I'm looking forward to comparing notes. Let me just grab something to eat before the lines get too long."

"Sure. I'll be here."

Yes, I know.

The New Hire walked over to the food section, noticing the crowd pile in at a steady pace. Maybe she could try to befriend a chatty stranger?

After filling her plate with a large bed of romaine lettuce, the New Hire evaluated her add-in options from the salad bar: grape tomatoes, an assortment of thinly sliced raw vegetables, a few less-healthy toppings (croutons, bacon bits, and shredded cheese), and several dressing choices. Feeling as if she lingered long enough, the New Hire made the dead man's walk back to her chair.

Approaching the table, the New Hire did a doubletake. She saw something that had so far eluded her. Miracles of miracles! The Tech Czar was talking to someone else. Far more shocking, not only did the conversation look friendly but also effortless.

Enormously careful not to intrude, the New Hire discreetly took her seat and began to eat.

"Please don't let me interrupt," she said, trying to finish her food as quickly as possible without giving herself heartburn.

"No worries. I want to introduce you to a former client of mine. We used to work together when I lived in Chicago. We probably haven't seen each other in nine years."

"Wow. Very nice. Well, I certainly don't want to stop the reunion. We'll be at the post-lunch session together, so we can talk then. Besides, I have phone calls to make. I'll let you two catch-up."

The New Hire was beyond relieved. She politely excused herself and left the dining area.

In the hallway, she grabbed a self-service coffee and roamed aimlessly to clear her head. She felt drained from spending all day listening to lectures and trying to converse with the Tech Czar. Keeping an eye on the time, she slowly made her way to the assigned room for the next speaker. The Tech Czar was sitting in the front row. The New Hire took the seat next to her, praying the talk would start early.

After the ambiguously relevant session, the pair had a fifteen-minute break before the next lecture began—another talk they would be attending together. During this brief respite, the New Hire made a beeline to the restroom and, to her horror, realized the Tech Czar had the same destination.

Could this day get any worse?

The New Hire despised getting stuck in the bathroom with anyone, especially coworkers. The noises, the mindless chitchat, and the inappropriate use of handicap-friendly stalls, where inevitably people sit to get comfortable.

What kind of society forces grown adults who may or may not know each other to use a giant bathroom together, all at the same time? There was no viable positive outcome. Absolutely barbaric!

Upon entering the bathroom, the New Hire purposely walked to the end of a long row of stalls, at least hoping to avoid proximity to the Tech Czar. Eager to exit the bathroom without delay, the New Hire was on edge. Sitting for just a moment, hoping for a few precious minutes of meditation, she sensed a disturbance in the space-time continuum. Of all the stalls in the stadium-sized bathroom, some stranger chose to sit down next to the New Hire.

Awful.

Emerging from the end of the large bank of stalls, the New Hire headed to the sinks. She proceeded to wash her hands methodically, noticing the Tech Czar did not even rinse hers. Sensing the look of utter distress on the New Hire's face, the Tech Czar confessed: "I only use Purell. It is more effective than soap."

Uh, is it? The New Hire was not convinced.

Once on the other side of the bathroom door, the Tech Czar made a point to take an exaggerated handful of free hand sanitizer.

* * *

As the first full day of the conference's content began winding down, prolonged and continued contact with the Tech Czar seemed inevitable. Once again, the two found themselves together in a group session.

Realizing she could not say no to a probable dinner invitation with her soon-to-be official boss, the New Hire felt all too familiar nervousness take hold. Declining a meal would be not only odd but also extremely ungrateful. A bad look. The right thought, but the wrong message. Plus, it could tip off the Tech Czar that the New Hire was not too keen on her.

When the final session came to an end, the Tech Czar said, "You should join me for dinner. We're having sushi off the Strip. I have a friend who lives in town, and she's meeting me at seven."

The New Hire ran through a few different scenarios in her head, but nothing seemed like a plausible or even reasonable excuse. Her best option was to set the stage for a quick exit.

"Yes, definitely. Thank you for the offer. Fair warning though, it's likely an early night for me. I'm really feeling the jet lag. Still, I'd love to have dinner with you and your friend."

"No problem at all. Why don't we head up to our rooms to get refreshed, and we can meet in the lobby in an hour?"

"Perfect."

Feeling somewhat mentally prepared, the New Hire met the Tech Czar as agreed after a short break. As they waited for the taxi to pick them up from the hotel's entrance, the two engaged in somewhat normal chitchat. The New Hire focused on asking the Tech Czar as many questions as she could—her favorite tactic. People loved to talk about themselves. Always.

The New Hire began her barrage of questions, keeping one eye on the ETA displaying on the driver's GPS.

"Remind me, what day did you say you arrived here? Do you spend a lot of time in Las Vegas? When were you here last? What did you think of the speakers today? Which was your favorite session? Did you look at the agenda for tomorrow?"

The Tech Czar did not disappoint. As predicted, she happily talked for the majority of the rideshare.

"I love Las Vegas. My wife and I come here at least every other month, if not more. Actually, we own a condo just off the Strip. We try to use it as often as we can, or we rent it out."

"Oh wow. That is a big commitment to Las Vegas! You must really love it here. When did you buy the condo?"

"Last year. It's really nice. That part of town is much quieter than the Strip. You're still close enough to enjoy all the nightlife, the theater, and the casinos. Since it's just an hour or so by plane from L.A., we come without much planning. We can usually leave the kid with her grandparents, and off we go."

"Fun."

"The grandparents live near us, so they usually take the kid whenever we ask."

The Tech Czar deflected most of the questions about the conference. Maybe she was off-the-clock and did not want to talk shop, but it was curious. While Las Vegas had a reputation as an adult playground, the Startup had paid for the pair to attend the conference. Presumably, their goal was to learn about the latest trends and apply their findings for the greater good.

Since the Tech Czar was clearly more comfortable chatting about herself, the New Hire was happy to oblige. Before long, they arrived at Sushi Roku.

The plan: Consume food in a sixty-to ninety-minute timeframe and under no circumstances commit to having drinks afterward.

To the New Hire's surprise, dinner turned out to be rather pleasant. The Tech Czar's friend was personable and, more importantly, talkative.

"So, how long have you two known each other?" the New Hire inquired.

"Oh, we go way back—at least ten years. I was working in marketing at one of the big casinos here in town. We used to do a lot of business together," the Friend responded.

"Yeah, and since I have a condo in town, we get together every few months," the Tech Czar added.

The New Hire was relieved to talk to someone else—anyone else.

As they got closer to the end of the meal, the New Hire started replanting the jet lag seed. She casually yawned and reminded the two old friends that she flew in from the East Coast the night before. While dinner was better than anticipated, the New Hire was anxious to leave. She told the pair she would grab an Uber back to the hotel.

Once in the parking lot and 100 percent removed from the sight line of the Tech Czar, the New Hire checked her phone. It was only a twenty-nine-minute walk back to the hotel and, of course, still relatively early. Ready to get a little exercise, the New Hire began her journey, careful not to be seen. Once a safe distance from the restaurant, she put on her wireless headphones.

Listening to John Lennon sing about days nobody told him there'd be, the New Hire began walking toward the flashing lights of the Strip, enjoying the particularly warm breeze. She savored the opportunity to decompress before another day of awkward conversations and an unclear purpose.

* * *

The last day of the conference. She made it. More than anything, the New Hire wanted to sit poolside and relax in the hotel's lazy river. She woke up especially early and left her suitcase with the concierge. She conducted a small recon mission and found a set of day lockers in the basement of the conference hall. The New Hire packed a go bag complete with a bathing suit, baseball cap, and ponytail holder.

Exhausted from spending most of the conference thinking of ways to avoid spending any additional time with the Tech Czar, the New Hire announced that her flight was scheduled immediately following the last speaker of the day. Not exactly true, but definitely a reasonable assumption.

Like the previous day's content, the final day was full of similarly blue-sky speakers. In between sessions, the New

Hire tried connecting the dots into a somewhat coherent, if not incomplete, company strategy. Reviewing her notes, however, the through line was vague. Unfortunately, the picture emerging was a random assortment of speakers talking about an even more random assortment of theoretical concepts with a questionable connection to the Startup's mission.

When the conference ended early, the New Hire had a twinge of panic. The Tech Czar approached her. "Hey, do you want to grab a drink before your flight? I have dinner plans, but since we finished early, I have time."

Caught slightly off guard, the New Hire replied, trying to act as nonchalant: "Thank you so much for the kind offer. I know you're spending the weekend here, but I really think I should get to the airport. My flight is on time, for now. You can never tell what the TSA lines are going to be like, especially in Vegas."

The New Hire walked with the Tech Czar toward the conference hall exit. They awkwardly said goodbye, and the New Hire expressed her enthusiasm for her first day in the office: "Well, thank you for everything. I'm really looking forward to starting officially. I'll go through my notes over the next few days and put together some ideas."

"Sounds good."

"Great. Thanks again. Enjoy the rest of your trip, and see you soon."

As she turned, the New Hire watched the Tech Czar walk into the casino. Patiently, she waited until she was sure the coast was clear. The New Hire doubled back toward the basement to retrieve her go bag. She put up her hair, strategically pulled down a baseball hat exceptionally low, and changed in an out-of-the-way bathroom she had scoped out earlier that day.

The New Hire spent forty-five minutes unwinding by the pool. She knew it was risky. What if she ran into the Tech Czar? How could she begin to explain her deception? She was on high alert, but at least she was alone. Voluntary silence. The New Hire knew she should have just headed to the airport and sat for hours waiting for her flight. Anything would have been preferable to the Tech Czar's unique brand of torture. Instead, she chose the lazy river. She wanted to get something useful out of the conference.

With less than a week until her official start date, the New Hire reflected on her time in Las Vegas. She struggled to understand why a brand-new startup would spend three thousand dollars for her to attend a rather pointless conference, particularly since she was in a strategy role, not a technical one.

Even though the company had made a sizeable expenditure for the New Hire to attend the sessions, no actual or applicable work was required. Feeling uneasy, she wrote the Tech Czar an email reiterating her excitement about her soon-to-be-official job and a few of the key learnings from her experience. Unbeknownst to her, Las Vegas would be the last time the New Hire or the Tech Czar would ever substantially discuss the conference again.

While the Tech Czar made her uncomfortable, the New Hire was committed to making the situation work. In their brief time together, it had become abundantly clear the Tech Czar had no idea what her role was supposed to be, let alone anyone else's.

CHAPTER 3

LAWLESS AVENUES

Her first official day in the Startup's offices. Almost a week had passed since the New Hire had attended the mission-critical conference at the Founder's bequest. After sitting through more than a dozen lectures and spending two-and-a-half days with the Tech Czar, the New Hire had one takeaway: She had no idea what to expect next.

The Chief Happiness Officer welcomed her at the entrance. A laptop awaited with a yellow Post-it note detailing her username and password. The New Hire sat directly across from Happiness, who stacked reams of Xerox paper on their shared table to create an improvised divider. The New Hire didn't mind. Staring at someone all day is awkward—especially someone you didn't know.

The Tech Czar had not arrived yet, but it was still early. Pleasantly surprised by a fairly robust checklist of things to do, the New Hire dug in. Passwords to create, accounts to sign-up for, and mandatory videos to watch. Basic instructions on filing expenses, which software did what, and an overly comprehensive guide to using the printer.

A printer? Did companies still even have those?

She spent the first hour getting accesses sorted, customizing preferences, and setting up her desk. A mobile phone charger, a promotional mug from a popular streaming service television show, and her well-worn notebook. The New Hire placed a souvenir statue of Queen Elizabeth next to her monitor—a subtle nod to not only her hard-earned dual citizenship but also her time at the Search Engine.

The New Hire filed her expenses for reimbursement. She had spent several thousand dollars in Las Vegas. The event entrance fee. Last minute airfare. Multiple nights at a semi-luxurious hotel. Transportation. Incidentals.

Although she had actively tried to avoid the Tech Czar at the conference, the New Hire was ready to embrace her strategy role and Startup life. From her recently activated company email, she sent the Tech Czar a note hoping to arrange a time to meet. The New Hire was eager to discuss her core duties and responsibilities. Always conscientious, she wanted to make a good impression and prove her value.

Considering it was the New Hire's first day in the office, she assumed the Tech Czar would want to meet early morning to plan the day. The pair, however, sat on opposite ends of the office, even though the New Hire reported to her.

After an hour or two of admin work, the New Hire needed to stretch her legs. Four distinct sections separated the office: the front, the main, the theater (usually reserved for large meetings), and the back, which housed the former wardrobe rooms where she had interviewed. The New Hire sat in the furthermost row of seats in the main space, closest to the kitchen cutout.

The prominent retailer's former headquarters could have been straight from Central Casting. The perfect set location for an up-and-coming Startup. Open-plan seating. Cheap but practical furniture. An assortment of unusual characters. Unless television and movies had lied to her, this is what startups were supposed to be like. Or, at least, what they were supposed to *look* like.

In the front, by the visitor's entrance, there was a small bank of desks. The Tech Czar and IT team had set up shop there. The New Hire walked toward this area, but they were still not in the office yet.

Around the corner felt like a different world. It was the heart of the office and where most folks congregated. Writers, graphic designers, app developers. A wide-open space anchored by the small galley kitchen and a table of trendy, free snacks. Vegetable chips, upmarket animal jerkies, and high-end chocolates.

The Office Manager would occasionally supplement the monthly delivery with childhood favorites: Ruffles, Doritos, Cheetos, Fritos, Flavored Lays. By the end of the day, the Frito-Lay Classic Mix would be gone, leaving behind their organic counterparts.

In the main area, up to three ergonomic chairs filled every row. Monitors placed socially distant. In the middle of each table was a massive power strip, loaded with everything, and anything, to charge personal devices.

As the day progressed, the floor began to fill with people. Many were either milling around or glued to their laptops. There were no introductions. The New Hire appeared as a fact, and the rest of her now-new colleagues seemed to accept this change as a reality.

Trying to be proactive, she scheduled a meeting with the Project Manager to get better visibility into operations. The PM declined her invitation.

The Tech Czar had worked previously at a well-known academic university. The New Hire could tell. She was not driven by return on investment metrics, improving inefficiencies, or hitting goals like most technology workers.

Instead, the Tech Czar loved nothing more than to talk about her unit, her people. Her current team included a loyal group of followers, all collected from previous companies. In the short time the New Hire had observed her, it was apparent she placed an outsized importance on her leadership skills—and her ability to motivate others.

At the conference, in one of her more animated moments, the Tech Czar spoke about her time working for the University.

"You know, life at these private colleges can be very challenging, especially for these young kids. Most find it really hard to manage critical feedback. I was one of the few members of staff who had a gold star on her door."

"A gold star?"

"Oh, yeah. The University created a system to indicate to students that my office was a safe space. A space where they could feel their feelings. Students were free to come to me and be open about any aggressions they felt."

"Huh. Interesting. What does that mean? A safe space?"

"Well, I was an ally to any student who needed a safe adult to talk about really anything, free from judgment or bias. I would really just listen and validate their feelings."

This revelation was almost incomprehensible to the New Hire. So, included with their yearly seventy-thousand-dollars-plus sticker price tuition bill, kids could monologue to a carefully curated adult about all of the injustices of the world? Yes, life was unfair, but probably less so when your parents are paying your way. Wasn't it more than a little cruel to create this bubble for students? Most people couldn't care less about others and their problems—especially the problems of a coworker.

The Tech Czar mentioned this gold star so frequently at the conference, the New Hire was sure she would find one at the Startup. While the badge system seemed completely and totally irrelevant in the real world, the New Hire thought it was a perfect example of how disconnected the Tech Czar was from working in the for-profit sector. Academia was perhaps a better fit for her rather than the winner-take-all mentality of Big Tech.

Around 10:30 a.m., the Stepdaughter arrived. The New Hire surmised this from her limited conversations with new colleagues. The common refrain around the proverbial water cooler was something to effect of: "Oh, yes, the Founder's Stepdaughter works here."

She floated across the wide-open space, carrying a large Birkin bag, a supersized Hydro Flask, and textbooks used for schoolwork. Unlike the rest of her coworkers, the Stepdaughter greeted the staff as she made her way to her desk. She seemed genuine not only in her approachability, but also in her interest in others. She was quick to introduce herself to the New Hire.

"Welcome! We're glad you are here."

The two exchanged pleasantries, and then the Stepdaughter promptly sat on the other side of the large lunch table, next to Happiness.

Only Happiness and the Stepdaughter could see the whole of the office from where they sat. Or at least the majority of the office. They could not see around the corner where the IT group was holed up.

Since the New Hire sat directly across from Happiness and the Stepdaughter, her back faced most staff. At the opposite end of the main space, the VP sat, also observing the hive of activity in the middle.

The New Hire did not fully understand why she was sat directly across from Happiness. She always seemed in the middle of something. Even when she arrived in the morning, Happiness was mid-conversation. Since she wore discreet wireless headphones, it was challenging to figure out if she was talking to herself or actually on the phone. The New Hire would occasionally overhear a family conversation with her presumably teenaged children and unintentionally catch overly prescriptive directions on what they were supposed to do after school.

Happiness was standoffish and seemed to intimidate her colleagues. From sheer proximity, the New Hire could hear Happiness constantly whispering with the Stepdaughter. The New Hire tried to be unobtrusive. She wasn't the type to listen in on other's conversations.

Over time, the New Hire would grow to like not only the Stepdaughter, but also Happiness sincerely. While at first unsure about the seating arrangement, she enjoyed sitting close to the action. Before long, the trio realized how much they all had in common. Perhaps, the New Hire had found some allies?

* * *

By late morning, the Tech Czar finally responded to the New Hire's request to meet and indicated she was available later in the day.

"It is nice to see you again, and thank you for taking the time to meet. I'm not sure where you want to start, but we can review some of my notes from the conference, or I can tell you what I have been working on so far."

"Yes, I saw you sent through some notes, but I have not had a chance to review them yet. Let's start with today, and we can discuss the conference at another time."

The Tech Czar was distracted. Disinterested even. The New Hire had flashbacks to her interview. To avoid either more awkward silence or assignments she did not want to complete, two things she hated, the New Hire knew she had to take the lead. She felt confident pushing her own agenda from their limited experiences together.

The New Hire began filibustering: "Great, well, I'm working through the first day checklist. It's immensely thorough, so thank you for that. I have requested all the accesses I need and watched a number of the training videos already. Today, I'm focusing on the easy stuff. In the afternoon, I can start meeting some folks to review where we are with development. I want to make sure I really understand what the objectives are and what has been done so far. Once I wrap my head around everything, maybe my first project should be an audit of where we are? I'm thinking just a top-line view of what's working and what's not. I can make recommendations on where we might want to streamline processes."

"I like that idea. It sounds good."

Confirming what she suspected, the New Hire recognized the Tech Czar did not have a plan for her. With very little understanding of the product they were building, the New Hire decided what her priorities should be.

As she settled into her first week, the New Hire completed the entire checklist of admin tasks. She explored the shared drive, looking for background information on the project. She found the business plan, an investor presentation, and old strategy decks. The New Hire read through whatever previous documentation she could find.

Feeling, in theory, like she understood the team's objectives, the New Hire was ready to learn more about the overall status. She scheduled time with the VP to dig into specifics.

"Good morning, and thank you for your time today. It's been a busy few days. I reviewed most of the documentation on the shared drive, so I am starting to wrap my head around our goals and objectives. It would be great to hear your take. I'd love your thoughts on where we are, what still needs to be done, and how I can help push the project forward," the New Hire said kicking off the meeting.

"Definitely. I'm excited you're here. Let me give you a little background on how the process works. Design is working on the wireframes for the final prototype based on my direction. We have gone through several strategy changes over the last eighteen months. All around the office, you can see the evolution of the project," the VP replied

The office was engulfed in a tsunami of printed pages. Mountainous stacks of paper either covered the VP's desk or were taped on the wall around her. Blue-sky concepts. Page mock-ups. Mobile architecture. All works in progress. The VP loved to print everything. Anything. The New Hire could see the value of sometimes seeing the art on paper, but at a certain point, there was no point. They worked in an online world. Designs should be evaluated in their native formats.

Continuing, the VP said, "Before you started, we set up a War Room. For a week, we all gathered in the theater for eight hours a day to nail down priorities and the roadmap. We are now more or less coalesced around what the final strategy will be. Currently, my team is building the Beta, and then I need to approve everything."

"I see. So, what's the main blocker?"

"The team is waiting on final signoff from the Founder."

"Got it. Can you send me your Go-to-Market Plan and a list of things you need to ensure we can get the prototype built?"

"I'm still working on the marketing materials. I'll send you my wish list, though."

The New Hire was surprised the VP did not have a Go-to-Market Strategy completed. It seemed an important first step to launching a new product. Nonetheless, from what she could tell, the most crucial ingredients to building a great app were there. Writers. Graphic designers. App developers. The staff lacked direction and a plan. Presumably, this was why the New Hire was hired. She was skilled at operationalizing teams and adding the structure necessary to turn theory into reality.

The New Hire believed in radical honesty. In her mind, she did not believe the Tech Czar or the VP would be surprised if her analysis found something amiss. Not having a fully functioning Mobile App after eighteen months of development was too long. Way too long. The teams were ready to execute, but they needed clarification on what that execution should be.

After their initial meeting, the New Hire struggled to get more time on the VP's calendar.

"I'm so sorry, but I have to work on the brand style guide. Can you send me an email?" the VP proclaimed as she rushed her way through the office.

The New Hire sent over a bulleted list of observations but could not get a response from the VP. Unable to get her feedback, the New Hire determined the best course was to get something visual in front of the Tech Czar. She created two slides to illustrate her conclusions and point of view. She scheduled time to review.

TIMELINE

Bright Start, But Nothing Tangible

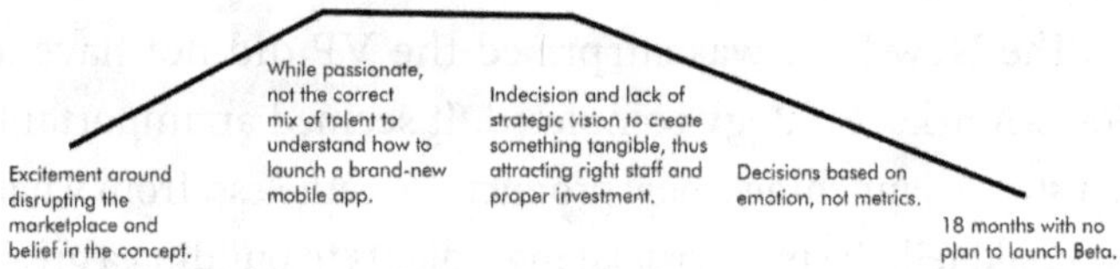

REBOOT

Course Correction, But Still Fundamental Issues

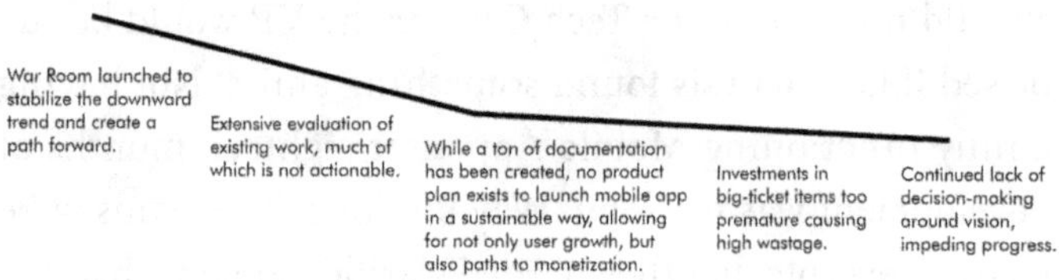

"Thank you for meeting with me. As previously discussed, I have been working on putting together a high-level analysis of where I think we are in terms of development. Essentially, it's an executive summary for you.

"I wanted to keep it to just two slides, covering the timeline and the reboot a few months ago with commentary on what our next steps should be. I met with the teams to get a feel for what is working and what could use some improvement.

"I also reviewed the business plan and several other decks I found on the shared drive. Overall, I am very impressed with the team's passion and commitment. I think we're making real progress, which is great news. I have identified a few stumbling blocks, and there is definitely an opportunity to streamline a few things.

"From what I have gathered, I think we should focus on three main priorities:

1. Sticking to decisions already made;
2. Simplifying the approval process; and
3. Finding more efficiency on big expenditures."

Taking a beat to review the slides, the Tech Czar replied, nervously laughing, "It looks like your analysis is saying I should be fired! Ha ha."

The New Hire faintly smiled, but that was exactly what she thought.

Trying to wrap up the discussion and move forward, the New Hire added, "So, what are the next steps?"

"Well, the Founder needs to approve any strategic decisions."

"Okay, when do you think we could get on his calendar?"

"Let me get back to you."

Several weeks passed. Inaction. The New Hire reevaluated her priorities. She knew the executive summary was the right plan to move forward but decided to back burner her ideas. Not even two weeks on the job, she still lacked the influence to implement any changes. Instead, she would focus her attention on putting together a review of the competitive landscape. Insights would be a much easier sell—at least for now.

* * *

The site that housed the Startup was an eclectic mix of five distinct buildings, each reflecting different boom-and-bust periods in Hollywood. Over time, these high-rises became connected by convenience, not design. After several days of taking the elevator to the lobby, exiting onto the street, and walking around the block to get to her car, a coworker showed the New Hire a secret pathway through the building. Employees could enter from the sixth floor of the parking structure and travel an entire city block indoors through an elaborate maze of corridors, ramps, and hallways.

Build in the 1930s, much of the building's interior remained true to its original intent. When exiting the visitor's entrance, a small communal bathroom was available across from the stairwell. An employment agency also occupied the same floor as the Startup and provided a continual stream of women who simultaneously always needed to use the restroom. When lines started to form to use the mere three available stalls, the New Hire would grow agitated. Deep down, she felt there was something fundamentally wrong with waiting to use the bathroom at her workplace. This was not the intermission of *Hamilton*.

The New Hire believed very deeply the work bathroom should be a sanctuary. A place to get away. Escape. Even if only for a moment or two. Plus, she hated getting stuck in the bathroom with other women. If unavoidable, she did not mind strangers. She would never see them again. *But coworkers? What if you are sitting inches away from someone who may or may not be responsible for your performance review? Gross.*

The image of the Tech Czar choosing not to wash her hands with soap and water in Las Vegas was seared in the New Hire's memory. She did not want to get trapped in another uncomfortable situation. She chose to avoid the seventh-floor bathroom altogether.

The New Hire would routinely see the Tech Czar through the glass doors, returning from a pit stop, pausing at the Office

Manager's desk for the briefest squirt of company-provided Purell. She imagined the Tech Czar, proud of her defiance of societal norms, marking her territory along the way, touching the bathroom door and the Startup entrance with unwashed hands, only stopping for a courtesy pump perhaps because there was an audience.

Out of necessity, the New Hire needed to find a private bathroom and spent her downtime searching various floors of the high-rise. She appreciated her surroundings. The spectacular architecture. The beauty. The historical significance. Building exploration soon became a favorite activity. As a bonus, she could get some exercise and complete these discovery assignments in solitude.

Having few responsibilities and unimpressed with her boss's attitude toward work and personal hygiene, the New Hire grew restless. She had trouble adjusting to the slower pace of the Startup. While eager to push through her ideas to streamline processes, she knew to wait for the right opening.

In the meantime, the New Hire tried to limit her interactions considerably with the Tech Czar. Sitting near the kitchen and the free food made this operation highly improbable.

"Hey there. How are you? I feel like we haven't had a chance to talk much," the Tech Czar said, catching the New Hire debating between Cool Ranch Doritos and Sour Cream and Onion Ruffles.

"I'm good. Yes, I feel like I'm making traction. I'm working on an overview of the state of search. There are quite a few interesting trends and features I'd like to highlight. We should explore a few possibilities for the Beta."

Disconnected from the actual conversation, the Tech Czar said, "Yeah, yeah. Listen, I'm simply a vessel. My purpose is to help you succeed."

Trying to be polite, the New Hire listened, thinking, *I have seen this tree before*, as her boss continued down this well-worn path.

"I want you to know how serious I am. I think you have huge potential. My job is to give you the opportunity to grow."

Then, for no apparent reason, the Tech Czar cocked her head to the side and spat a loogie onto the already dirty, brown carpet.

Shocked and horrified, the New Hire looked at the Tech Czar. Out of instinct, she exclaimed: "What's happening?"

The New Hire had a true concern. Was this a medical emergency? Should she call 9-1-1? The Tech Czar continued with her monologue as the New Hire's eyes stayed fixated on the wet spot.

"As I was saying, I want you to be happy here. I want you to do well."

Does she think what just happened was socially acceptable behavior? They are inside. At a place of business. At their place of business. She spit. Intentionally. This was not the result of over-animation or excitement. A mistake, where while telling a story, something regrettably, uncontrollably, flies from one's mouth. Or an accident. No. This was a choice. A decision. Deliberate.

As the Tech Czar continued, the New Hire knew an excuse and, more importantly, an apology would not be forthcoming.

The New Hire was distressed, but the Tech Czar remained undeterred. She persisted with her speech as if nothing happened: "I am here for you. My goal is to enable your success. My platoon always succeeds."

The New Hire felt gaslit. *Did she just see what she thought she saw?*

Then, the Tech Czar spit. Again. A second time. She turned her head and let more saliva and mucus fly out of her mouth.

This time, the New Hire lost her patience: "Really?"

The Tech Czar rebutted with a half-hearted response, "Oh, sorry."

Although she had never been a big Gordon Lightfoot fan, "Carefree Highway" was on loop in the New Hire's head. She heard the distinctive melody and the chorus refrain. Ironically, she didn't really even know the words to the song but seemed to remember there was something about slipping away and better days. Was this the last-chance saloon?

CHAPTER 4

PEOPLE ARE STRANGE

At work, the New Hire always knew what to do. She was self-assured and confident. She could make decisions with ease and never look back. Never think twice about it. The New Hire loved taking risks. When she did make a mistake, it was a learning opportunity. A chance to reflect. To pivot. To course-correct. Consequences were inconsequential. Repairable. At each turn, there was another do-over. A reset.

Several weeks into the Startup gig, the New Hire realized most of the staff were not overly busy. In fact, she wasn't that busy. *Was it cyclical?* She figured the workload would come, especially as they got closer to production and releasing the Mobile App.

The New Hire focused on nailing down who the key players were and what they contributed to the Startup. The overall team consisted of a mix of creative and technical folks. The app developers reported to the Tech Czar, along with technology specialists. The VP had a team of designers and content producers. There was the Director of Sales, but no actual sales. And while the team was working on building a product, there was no Product team.

The New Hire was most intrigued by the Stepdaughter. It was unclear what exactly she did, but it seemed to occupy a large chunk of her time. She also possessed two qualities that made her distinctive from the other employees. She was friendly and outgoing. It was a relief when the New Hire talked to her.

"How are you settling in so far?" the Stepdaughter asked, expressing legitimate interest.

"Good. I only feel slightly overwhelmed."

"I bet. I know the feeling. This schoolwork is killing me."

"Yes, your textbooks give you away. What are you studying?"

"I just started my PhD. Funny, huh? Working toward a degree in food science while moonlighting here? It's true, though. Before too long, I'll become a doctor of food. I'm in a somewhat condensed but flexible program. They try to jam everything they can into the shortest time humanly possible. I'm learning a ton, but I fantasize about having some free time. School's all I do."

"How much more do you have left?"

"Just over two years, ha ha. I know, I am barely through the program, and I'm already complaining."

"I get it. Doctorate programs are tough. It's very admirable, especially with a full-time job."

"Right? Also, my boyfriend has a two-year-old son. Yep, I know. A two-year-old. Oh, and long-story-short, he mostly lives with us. Don't ask. I love him, obviously, but he's a handful. I definitely feel it. Time is tight, but it's temporary. At least that's what I tell myself."

The Stepdaughter clearly had a lot on her plate, but the New Hire admired her. She was industrious and exuded positivity, focus, and drive. The New Hire felt better knowing there might be someone in the office to whom she could relate. Or, at the very least, respect her work ethic.

* * *

As the New Hire tried to memorize names and titles, another worrisome thought crossed her mind. A month had passed, and she had yet to receive any payment for services rendered.

Didn't Happiness say payday was every two weeks? Maybe she misremembered. Was it monthly? Perhaps her official first day was too close to the end of the pay period. Could there have been an unusual amount of paperwork that took time to process? She did not want to jump to conclusions without facts, but a narrative was emerging.

While obviously receiving the agreed-upon salary was important to the New Hire, she also had shelled out three thousand dollars for the Las Vegas boondoggle. She submitted her expenses on her first official day, following the well-documented procedures, but was still not reimbursed. Although she wasn't someone who lived paycheck to paycheck, the math was not in her favor. The amount going out of her bank account every two weeks was exceeding the amount coming in.

The New Hire contemplated how best to address the lack of pay. The Tech Czar was her boss. Her squad leader. Her commander in chief. Her advocate. She would schedule a one-to-one and ask the question. Believing being direct was always the best play, the New Hire would stick to the facts. The Tech Czar, so enthralled with her own leadership skills, would want to resolve this clear oversight quickly.

"Hey, I'm not sure if you are aware, but I haven't gotten paid yet. I think I have missed two payroll cycles. Also, I haven't received reimbursement for my expenses from the conference."

The Tech Czar immediately deflected. "The Stepdaughter handles all payroll issues. Talk to her and drop the Founder a note."

Her retort astonished the New Hire. Fair enough if the Stepdaughter handles payroll issues, but typically, a supervisor would more actively manage an administrative issue, especially if money was involved. The New Hire was happy to talk to the Stepdaughter but reaching out directly to the Founder seemed extreme. At this point, she had never had a direct conversation with him. Also, isn't this what he paid people to handle for him?

Hitting a dead end with the Tech Czar, the New Hire approached the Stepdaughter. Trying to diffuse the situation, the New Hire asked over the desks. "Oh, hey. I just wanted to let you know I haven't received my first paycheck yet. Or second. I'm sure it's just a setup issue, but I thought I would flag it as it has been a month."

The Stepdaughter seemed genuinely bewildered. She had the same misplaced guilt of a lender forced to ask a borrower to return that thing they borrowed. "Oh no. Really? I apologize. Let me look into that right away. I'll get this fixed ASAP."

The New Hire trusted the Stepdaughter. She was straightforward and direct. If the Stepdaughter said she would rectify the situation, she would. Within the week, the New Hire was paid all the money she was owed—her salary and expenses. Case closed.

With her pay now sorted, the New Hire mentally made a running list of the oddities, curiosities, and bizarre things she had witnessed in her short tenure at the Startup. She expected the eccentric personalities but was stunned by the lack of drive and initiative to release the Beta version.

Once or twice a week, an older man would show up in the offices, causing a flurry of activity. The New Hire presumed this individual to be the company Founder. He was mentioned briefly in the interview, but there was no introduction so far.

She had interviewed with the Chief Happiness Officer, VP, and Tech Czar, but they all took direction from the Founder. The New Hire needed to learn more about him.

Feeling somewhat settled in her role, she had developed a rapport with the creative team. Catching the Lead Designer in the kitchen, the New Hire gently prodded. "So, I guess the Founder usually works from home?"

"No, he works from his Shared Workspace Solutions Company."

"Oh. That's a fun fact. I didn't even realize he owned a Shared Workspace Solutions Company."

"Yep, that's his profession. He does office workplace development. The Startup is his side gig. I heard he had this kooky dream last year and became fixated on building a mobile app. Since everyone is trying to reach Gen Z these days, he decided that's who he should target. And, just like that, presto! Here we are trying to build an app to find that audience. I guess he did do some research and felt there was a gap in the marketplace. Who knows? I am not sure how true the story is, but that's what I have heard."

Other business? A Shared Workplace Solutions Company? Creating an entirely unique digital experience for young adults did not seem like a natural fit for someone who negotiates corporate housing deals for a living.

Equally as strange, the Shared Workplace Solutions Company was located just up the street from the Startup. A mere ten-minute journey by foot. Whenever the Founder summoned any of his Executive staff, they would drive, valet their cars, and expense forty-eight dollars.

Even though the Founder worked offsite, he definitely was not hands-off. His vision drove the company and his leadership team. At first glance, the New Hire wouldn't have necessarily noticed him. His clothes matched his overall demeanor—well-worn. Just like the Startup's office space, he looked tired.

His button-down shirt had out of style lapels and large cuff links. The white color of his shirt was somewhat transparent, revealing a matching undershirt. The Founder wore predictably black/brown slacks and orthopedic-friendly shoes. Add a matching belt and his outfit looked like standard issue from those movies about G-men with capped salaries.

When the New Hire looked closer, however, a flash of gold caught her eye. His watch was definitely not standard issue. Certainly not an expert by any means, as she didn't even own a watch, but the logo was instantly identifiable.

The Founder wore a Rolex. A statement piece. From the way the light hit the watch, it did not look like a fake, but the New Hire could not be sure. From what she surmised, the Founder walked around the office in nondescript attire and what looked like a somewhat sizable down payment on his right wrist.

As the team inched toward Beta, the Founder would ebb and flow into the Startup's offices more frequently. Even more unusual than his seemingly expensive timepiece and incongruent style of dress was that neither the Tech Czar nor anyone else for that matter had formally introduced the New Hire to the Founder. Almost two months had passed since her start date. She missed her opportunity to introduce herself.

None of the usual rituals assumed in a professional working environment were in place at the Startup. No regularly scheduled team meetings, no weekly one-to-ones, and no push to get things done. When the Founder emerged, the office would whip into a frenzy. All hands on deck. Sound the alarm and drop everything. The goal was to react and follow orders, not think and ask why. He would pull together an all-employee meeting in the theater without warning. Like any natural disaster, staff sought shelter from wherever they were.

The Founder's company-wide meetings were disorganized, rambling, and urgent. He seemed frustrated the project did not have a direction or a path forward. Of course, he surrounded himself with people waiting for his blessing. The Founder talked about his vision and how the team was building the next hot destination Mobile App for Gen Z. During these meetings, he would infect the Executive team with language they would then repeat back for weeks.

"We need a North Star. Our Mobile App will become part of the urban ecosystem. We are about diversity at all levels of content, opinion, and social economics. We democratize play for providers and users. This Startup always will directly challenge the homogeny of existing companies and multinational conglomerates that currently dominate the industry," the Founder stated emphatically.

Afterward, the VP and Tech Czar would parrot "North Star" or "homogeny" nonsensically into most conversations.

Everyone in the office would sit slightly on edge as the Founder would direct. Commands were given in lists: Do this. Do that.

The Founder dictated, "This is your only priority. I want you to stop working on everything else until this is done."

Since he changed his mind so frequently, these simple directions were difficult to execute. The New Hire observed a distinct pattern of the Founder floating into the team's orbit, ordaining the chosen ones with his attention or point of view, and then just as stealthily drifting out, leaving the others to decipher his code.

As a follow-up, a smaller group, including the New Hire, the Stepdaughter, the VP, and Tech Czar would meet to develop an execution plan. These meetings, however, usually resulted in more chaos. The VP tended to have a unique take on the direction given. She often boasted, "Well, based on my private conversations with the Founder, I think this is what he really meant." The VP relished her alleged Batline more than whatever the Founder had instructed the team to do.

These impromptu sessions gave the New Hire a chance to get to know the Stepdaughter better. Without any prior discussions, regardless of the topic, they always seemed to be aligned.

"I was reading back through the Founder's email, and I think he wants us to change tact," the VP would predictably say.

Chiming in, the Tech Czar offered: "Pookie is right."

"Hmm. That's not quite what I got from the note. At the end of the day, we have to get a minimum viable product out the door so we can start testing. Until we have something tangible, we don't have any data. The sooner we get something—anything—out the better. We can always go back, iterate, and make changes. Without any customer input, we are in a vicious loop," the New Hire countered.

"Exactly. The priority is to get to market and see what folks think. I can confirm, though," the Stepdaughter said while quickly sending a text message to the Founder.

Seeing a chance to hedge, the Tech Czar added, "Well, yeah. I mean, I guess we need to get something out, sooner rather than later."

Despite the consensus, the VP loved to cast doubt. She would concur with the group, waiting for the Founder to give his blessing. On cue, she would then schedule a one-to-one meeting to try to change his mind. It was unclear if the

Founder legitimately agreed with the VP or was just exhausted by her dogged nature. Her goal: control the vision.

The New Hire knew to stay above the fray. Getting involved in who controlled what was a familiar trap. The VP, whom the New Hire was so fond of during the interview, was someone to watch. Always friendly to her face, she relished the snide aside. It was a compulsion. Mid-conversation, the VP usually could find a way subtlety to put someone down. At first, the New Hire did not notice much, but frequent comments like, "Well, that's not what I would have done!" punctured by an obnoxious laugh, began to stick.

Like a predator scoping out her prey, the VP was casting her net. She was looking for followers. Followers to join her faction in her quest to run the project. Of course, once they no longer served her purpose, she would toss them aside like a used carcass.

Her favorite victims: the designers. Due to their proximity to her desk, she would often stop by for a second opinion.

"What do you guys think of this new direction? It's a total step backward, right?"

Without any context, someone on her team would eventually offer a half-hearted confirmation to her inquiries: "I guess. Yeah, sure. Okay."

The VP would use these less than full-throated endorsements to circle back with the Founder and prove her way of thinking. If the VP ran into resistance she could not overcome, she quickly would blame Design for their poor guidance.

More frequently than not, the New Hire was running damage control. Her goal was to get the Beta released. Since the Stepdaughter appeared to have the same objective, the New Hire tested the waters. "Yikes. Sometimes, I feel like people want to keep us in this continual cycle of tweaking what has already been done. I thought we were here to launch something."

"Girl, are you just figuring that out?"

"Ha ha. No. Please explain the dysfunction to me."

"Who knows? I just try to stay out of it."

"Yeah, I like that plan. Me too, then."

With similar ages and working histories, the New Hire and Stepdaughter were developing a bond. They looked forward to morning banter. With Happiness sitting in the same vicinity, it made sense that they all grew closer.

"Good morning, ladies," the Stepdaughter would announce, arriving in the office.

"Morning. How are you?" the New Hire would respond.

"I'm okay. Super tired today. I was up most of the night, though. My boyfriend is out of town, and he asked if I was willing to babysit. I stupidly said yes, not realizing this would be his son's first night without either of his parents. It was a nightmare. So much negotiation. Boy, I'll never agree to that again!"

"Oh no. Did your boyfriend know that?"

"He claims he didn't. Sounds suspicious to me."

"Me too."

"Well, do you know what my kids did? They somehow managed to flood the bathroom! How? I don't know," Happiness chimed in.

"What do you mean? Like, water on the floor, or water through the ceiling?" the New Hire asked.

"Which one do you think?"

"Ha ha. Oh man, that's horrible. What did you do?"

"What could I do? I made the kids clean up as much of the water as possible. I don't have a dry towel in the house.

I must've run the dryer all night. I have a contractor friend coming over tonight to see what he recommends."

"That sounds ominous."

"All I know is whatever the fix, it will be more than I want to pay."

* * *

The New Hire continued to spend her days assigning herself research projects. While her full analysis of how to move forward hadn't gained any traction, she stayed focused on investigating larger industry trends and tying it back to the Mobile App. At the minimum, she could add some value. The New Hire had a pretty good understanding of where development had stalled and how to accelerate whatever momentum they gained into an actionable plan. She knew to be patient. Her strategy was solid, but the timing was not right.

Waiting for a more inopportune time to start proposing ideas, the New Hire grew more curious about not only the people she was working with but also the building itself. During an all-staff meeting, the Founder referred to expanding out the office. He mentioned renovating up to two additional floors. Since the current staff took less than one-third of their current space, this seemed like an unusual expenditure.

During her interview, Happiness mentioned the Founder owned several floors in the building, and they were remodeling the one downstairs. *Didn't she? Ripe for expansion, right?* Had the New Hire imagined that conversation?

Every day, walking to and from her car through the maze of hallways, corridors, and ramps, the New Hire had passed a closed door with a written notification. *Was that the remodeled offices? It must be.* Since the Founder owned a Shared Workspace Solutions Company, she imagined he kitted out the space nicely. Maybe she would take a closer look during lunch.

Making her way down a flight of stairs, the New Hire felt a slight rush of adrenaline. She could hear Carly Simon's refrain: "Anticipation…."

She headed toward the other side of the building, where the lower floor connected directly to the parking structure. She approached the door with the posted piece of paper taped in the window. Looking around, the New Hire evaluated her surroundings. She was confident the area was free from unsuspecting eyes, including electronic ones.

By instinct, she placed her hand on the handle, assuming it was locked. It wasn't. If the door was unlocked, surely there wouldn't be much harm in looking around, she thought.

She slowly opened the door.

More startlingly than the utter lack of security was the complete absence of any recent construction work. Viewing the space, she concluded some foundational work had been done at one point. The walls were exposed, with plastic covering filling in as temporary windows. An assortment of errant nails littered the cement floor. No tools were visible, but one of the state-mandated signs mentioned the importance of wearing a hard hat.

Where were the construction workers?

The New Hire did not know what to make of the quiet construction site. Like everything at the Startup, perhaps the team was waiting for feedback from the Founder. For now, just another Stranger Thing. Something to add to her ever-growing list of peculiarities.

CHAPTER 5

WORLD TURNING

After the initial payroll snafu, which caused a delay to the New Hire's first two checks and expense reimbursement, the Founder resolved all monetary issues. Or so she thought.

Staff received biweekly payments, but a troubling pattern began to emerge. Around the first or fifteenth of the month, the Founder would send an email stating the wire transfers were behind. Due to his varied personal and professional commitments or some sort of philanthropic engagement, either he unintentionally missed the filing deadline, or the bank was still handling the request.

Perhaps the Founder was disorganized? Instead of using an automated system, the Startup processed checks manually. Simply errors of omission. Harmless enough. The company was young and experiencing its teething pains. By the end of the month, the New Hire was receiving two paychecks. So what if they were sometimes late?

Without fail, the Founder would send a note to the team overexplaining the situation. His "Spontaneous Demonstrations held every week" emails became so ubiquitous, the New Hire barely skimmed the content. She found a strange comfort in his compulsion to rewrite the same message over and over again. Bottom line: unforeseen delay.

Late Friday afternoon, the New Hire received a familiar notification:

> **Subject: Important Update**
>
> Due to a clerical error, the payroll was just transferred. It was supposed to be distributed this morning. As a result, wires will not be seen in your accounts until Monday—most likely first thing. I am quite upset about this. As an apology, I have gifted an additional $750 to everyone for this unforeseen error. This will be reflected directly in your paycheck. Thank you for all your efforts over the last few weeks. Have a great weekend.

As her eyes scanned the mea culpa, the New Hire noticed an unexpected plot twist: an additional seven hundred and fifty dollars! Choosing not to question the sincerity of the Founder's motives, she was grateful for the unearned bonus. And a hefty one! She heard the O'Jays' chorus, loud and clear.

Despite these payroll glitches, the Startup did not appear plagued with money woes. Without a release date, however, there was no feasible way to generate revenue. The New Hire knew for the company to succeed, they had to streamline costs—not cut them completely but reduce where they could.

The Tech Czar, however, took the opposite approach. She continued to push the Founder to spend unnecessarily. Organizing a quick meeting, the Tech Czar promoted her latest scheme.

"We should invest in upgraded technology now. This means we can prepare now for further releases and have a backlog of features ready for post-launch. If we sign by this week, it's a real bargain. I negotiated a great deal. They will reduce their monthly fee by twenty percent and throw in free camera equipment. We need to sign this week, though, and commit to a six-month contract."

The Founder countered, "I'm not sure. Do you think we should be investing now? It does sound like a good deal."

Taking a second, the Tech Czar doubled down. "Well, the arrangement is only valid this week. If we drag our feet, we will lose the free camera gear. It is easily worth nine hundred dollars. That'll be ours to keep."

"It sounds tempting," the New Hire offered. "They've put together an attractive package and incentive, that's for sure. I'm getting stuck on the recurring fees, though. We're still months away from releasing. From what I remember, the monthly fee is fifteen grand? Even with a twenty percent reduced rate, that's a big chunk of change. We might be losing out on some top-notch camera equipment, but I think we should wait. Honestly, if they offer us the deal today, they will offer us the same deal down the line. Listen, the camera gear is exciting, but do we need it? I guess I'm missing what value it adds. We should table for now."

"Well, we are still gonna need to be prepared for future features right after we launch. We might as well purchase now, so we can start preparing. We can use the camera to do our own photo shoots," the Tech Czar said.

"Yes, the long-term plan should absolutely be to have a robust roadmap. But for phase one, shouldn't we just focus on building the minimum viable product? We're still missing user feedback and could be building features or enhancements our audience doesn't need or want. I know it's not ideal, but the focus has to be on the Beta and the path of least resistance. Also, I guess photo shoots will come in handy at some point, maybe when we start running advertising? Again, I think that's very far off into the distance."

Perhaps the New Hire missed the memo, but she was sure their jobs were not to spend money. Or, at the very least, not to spend money unwisely. The project was still in its infancy, so while it was important to dream big, ideas must be grounded in some reality. At each turn, the Tech Czar tried to invest in top-of-the-line project planning, customer relationship management, and automation tools. Why? They did not have a product, customers, or anything to track.

For a Chief Information Officer, the New Hire felt she had very little understanding of her role and, thus, the impact of her choices. Confirming many of her earlier suspicions, the Tech Czar was over her head. She did not know how to build things, and she certainly did not know how to create within a budget or deadline.

The more insight the New Hire got into the Tech Czar's decision-making process and work habits, the less she respected her. The Tech Czar loved coming in late and sneaking out early. Sometimes, as a cover, she would bring in her giant puppy. Having the dog with her was a great, seemingly innocent excuse for disappearing directly after lunch.

Half-Golden Retriever and half-standard Poodle, the Tech Czar's puppy was gigantic. The dog went by the name Kong, but the New Hire thought "Monster" more accurately described her bad behavior. She looked exactly like the luck dragon from *The Neverending Story.* Sweet by nature but completely untrained, the pup wreaked havoc in the wide-open spaces of the Startup.

The apple doesn't fall far from the tree.

Monster especially loved to pee on the once-vibrant couch near the main entrance. Brazen, the puppy wouldn't even bother to sneak away from her owner and do it privately. Monster would strut over, position her body near the edge of the couch, and relieve herself. When witnesses were present, the Tech Czar would half-hardly yell: "Kooong!" making zero attempts to clean up the urine. The New Hire never touched, sat, or went within ten feet of the couch.

Once, the New Hire ran into a Junior Designer walking toward the theater with paper towels and solvent. She instantly inquired, "What are you doing?"

"Oh, Kong had an accident. I guess she got over-excited. I was going to go pick up the poo before someone stepped in it."

"No, you're not. Is that your dog? No, it's not. Go tell the Tech Czar her puppy had an accident, and she needs to take care of it!"

The Junior Designer sheepishly agreed. As the New Hire turned away, she shouted: "And tell her she needs to use carpet cleaner!"

Several minutes later, the New Hire saw the Tech Czar walking toward the theater with a nondescript spray bottle and a wad of paper towels.

* * *

Days turned into a few months at the Startup, and the New Hire still felt an overall uneasiness about her job. While she was getting paid albeit a day or three late, what was her purpose for being there? As soon as she entered the office, the New Hire experienced a low-level rush of anxiety. Like a mild headache, she felt a dull pain persist throughout the day, clouding her thoughts. Apparently, she was not alone.

At least one employee called in sick every single day of the week. Statistically, that did not seem plausible.

Careful not to make a rash decision, the New Hire chose to take advantage of the company's unlimited vacation policy. A quick getaway. A rejuvenation. A chance to clear her head and refocus on her priorities. Two days off would do the trick. A long weekend to then come back refreshed. Recentered. Making an impact would not happen overnight. She continually reminded herself that the Startup had huge potential. This was the change she wanted.

On her second day out of the office, the New Hire received an unusual email from one of the app developers. While she would interact with some of the friendlier devs in the kitchen, there were limited day-to-day interactions. Not necessarily by choice, but the devs were building out functionality for a product that did not exist—at least not yet. The note read: "Congratulations on the promotion! You'll do a great job!"

Now, this was a mystery to the New Hire. *What promotion?*

Returning to the office the following week, the New Hire was mystified to see the Tech Czar's name appear on her phone. An incoming call. The Tech Czar had never called her before. Not only was it quite early in the morning, but also the pair were not calling friends. Or even friends.

The Tech Czar skipped courtesies and commenced into what was on her mind: "Needless to say, between my absence and yours, I'm not thrilled with how this discussion of a role transition has been handled."

The New Hire was confused. She had barely grabbed her first cup of coffee and could not understand what the Tech Czar was babbling on about. The New Hire felt like she woke up from a hangover and was trying to piece together the previous night, but everyone was talking too loudly.

Taking a deep breath, she said, "Can you take a step back? What happened? I was only out of the office for two days."

The Tech Czar sounded surprised. Breathing heavily from agitation, she continued: "The Founder didn't call you? Hearing your reaction, I can tell he didn't. Okay, so he gathered the staff for an impromptu all-hands meeting on Friday. You know how he likes to do that last minute. Well, I was sick, so I wasn't there either. But the gist is he wants you to lead the product team."

We have a product team? Shocked, the New Hire wasn't exactly sure what Product even did. Given the Tech Czar's reaction, she surmised it must be an expanded role. What she found even more unusual was the Founder chose her. She was quite confident he had no idea what she did.

The Tech Czar had never expressed much interest in anything relating to work, so clearly, somehow, this decision would impact her personally.

What could the other implications be? More money? Different responsibilities? An expanded focus on execution? Perhaps, a new reporting line? Maybe reporting directly to the Founder?

Angry, the Tech Czar's voice came across as if she was choking. Raising her voice, she bellowed, "We can still fix this!"

What was there to fix?

Sure, the New Hire didn't even know what the newly created role entailed, but the mere thought of no longer having to report to the Tech Czar was enough to pique her interest. Considering her current role was not taxing, a complete change might be what she needed. The New Hire knew how to turn ships around, and this one had to change course instantly. Icebergs ahead!

"I appreciate your thoughts. Thank you. And thank you for always looking out for me. My initial reaction, though, is this role is certainly worth considering," the New Hire responded.

Desperate not to lose her perceived power, the Tech Czar did not even try to hide her motives. She quickly tried to frame this new opportunity as insulting to the New Hire. "We weren't even there! He didn't even call you. There was no asking, just telling. I didn't want to interrupt your vacation, but I can help you figure out how to tell the Founder you don't want this role," she said.

Thinking about what the potential risks were, the New Hire could not anticipate many. Sure, she did not even know what a Head of Product did, but how hard could it be? She wouldn't know what the expectation would be of her. In fairness, the New Hire didn't know what was currently expected of her either.

The Tech Czar continued, "Okay, well, I'm not coming into the office today. The dog is still sick. I wanted to catch you on the phone, though. I should definitely be in the office tomorrow... I mean, barring any complications with Kong's health."

Obviously.

The New Hire did not want to blindside the Tech Czar, so she felt she should be honest (but not too honest). Testing the waters, she said, "Okay, well, thank you for the heads up. I definitely appreciate the concern, and I think you made some really valid points. I guess from my point of view, though, any opportunity, regardless of how poorly communicated, is worth exploring."

Undeterred, the Tech Czar continued with her argument but now taking on the role of savior. "Here's the thing: The Founder is unpredictable. I know how to manage him. I just wouldn't want you to have to deal with that."

The New Hire listened but stayed firm. "That's good feedback. I appreciate that. I really do. I guess I don't see the downside of trying a new role. I don't think people should turn down opportunities. Let me talk to the Founder and see what he has to say."

Within an hour, the Founder made his way to the Startup offices. The New Hire booked time with him in the green wardrobe room.

The Founder lead the chat. "Hey, listen, I'm sorry if there was any confusion with the new role. The Tech Czar said you were upset."

Of course she did.

"No, no. Not at all. I think she might have misinterpreted what I said. I was just surprised. Actually, I'm very excited about the role. It sounds like a great opportunity. I'd love to get some insight about your expectations."

"Easy. Launch the Beta in the next twelve months. That's it. One goal."

"Okay, that is certainly straightforward. Well, let me think about it, but I'm definitely up for the challenge. I won't let you down."

"Also, as this is a promotion, you'll receive a raise. Does that help convince you?"

While her mind was already made up, the New Hire was never one to turn down a sweetener. She expected a nominal raise but thought it was important to have a number in her head. Maybe there would be an opportunity to negotiate? A fifteen percent increase would be more than generous and exceedingly fair since she really had no idea what a Head of Product did.

"Yes, money always helps."

"I can pay you an extra four thousand a month," the Founder offered.

As this was a nearly thirty-five percent increase of her base, she did not even try to counter. The New Hire would move from her strategy role to become the Head of Product.

She was now part of the Executive team. Before the end of the week, she was reporting directly to the Founder.

Something had shifted. Approaching the end-of-year holidays, life at the Startup was changing for the New Hire. While she now had more power and influence, in some ways, her job was less complicated and more straightforward: get the product launched.

With her promotion, the Founder was now more determined than ever to release. The New Hire had given three months to the cause so far and saw no evidence of any progress. From what she had pieced together, in the year-and-a-half before her start date, there were zero signs of a viable product, idea, or much of a dedicated team. Oddly, none of this deterred the Founder. Full-steam ahead with the vision, even if he didn't know what that was. "We must move forward," he commanded often.

Conscious that the Founder usually started his day at 5:00 a.m., the New Hire tried to accommodate his schedule, within reason. He loved nothing more than to call the New Hire early in the morning with directives. Usually, these commands involved herding others and bringing them along, like accomplices, to the Shared Workspace Solutions Company's offices. Situated in a tall, white skyscraper on the hill looking down at the former retailer's headquarters, this second space was plush and ornate. A literal Ivory Tower. Among his favorites to pluck from their day-to-day activities into immediate crisis along with the New Hire: the Chief Happiness Officer and Stepdaughter.

These urgent meetings frequently involved company-changing directives. Mostly, the Founder had prechosen a path, but he loved to test his top lieutenants. He would pose questions that did not have answers. Typically, these conversations involved culling headcount, second-guessing previously decided decisions, or exposing something confidential about the staff—either revealing a salary or something said privately.

At times, the Founder would complain about specific employees. About the person he had hand-selected to be the creative head, he offered, "I'm going to cut his salary in half."

No longer shocked by the Founder's brutal and often inappropriate honesty, the New Hire tried to soften his stance. "Well, do you want to demote him? Or maybe you should just let him go if he is not delivering what you want? Or you could even give him a chance to step up and perform?"

"Nah, I think the pay cut will send the right message."

The New Hire did not see any value in pointing out this was not only illegal but also, morally, a terrible way to treat another human being. Instead of just taking the horse out back and putting it out of its misery, the Founder loved to keep all the broken-legged staff around. No hope of recovery. Since he would occasionally throw them a cash-laden bone framed as a bonus, he felt no remorse. The Founder simply did not acknowledge any suffering he caused.

"I'm thinking of letting go the developers and hiring an agency instead."

"Well, did you look at the numbers? What's the difference in cost between salaries and benefits versus outsourcing? Do you want to get rid of everyone? Or maybe keep someone internal to manage the agency?" Happiness piped in.

"Dear, that's what I pay you for. Can you please look into this and get back to me with a recommendation? Thank you."

"Yes, of course. I thought when we originally set up the team, we discussed the tradeoffs between using an in-house team and having an agency. I thought you decided you preferred hiring folks on-site."

"Please look into it again. Okay? Thank you."

The New Hire, Happiness, and Stepdaughter would always leave the Shared Workspace Solutions Company's offices in complete silence. Dazed and confused, they waited until the elevator doors had safely shut and their carriage was on its way down.

Shell-shocked, the New Hire said: "What just happened?"

"I don't know," Happiness replied.

"Don't look at me! Let's wait to see if any of this sticks. I guarantee he'll be distracted by something else by tomorrow. Shall we go to lunch?" the Stepdaughter offered.

"It might be too early for lunch. Breakfast?" Happiness said.

"Oh my god. I just had a filthy idea. Let's go to IHOP! It will be so gross, but it'll be so good!" the Stepdaughter declared.

"The International House of Pancakes! You had me at gross. Where is it?" the New Hire chimed in.

"By the Metro. Now, aren't you glad we have the car?" the Stepdaughter retorted.

"No. I would totally walk there. It's only ten minutes from here," the New Hire replied.

"Yes, from here, but then we would have to walk back from the restaurant to the other office. That's easily half an hour," the Stepdaughter pointed out.

"What? Thirty minutes? No way. I mean, maybe like twenty-five minutes. Or twenty-nine. Definitely, not thirty," the New Hire acquiesced while smiling.

"Also, you walk too much," the Stepdaughter added.

* * *

Occasionally, the Founder would summon the New Hire to his office individually. Always at the last minute, these one-to-ones were the Founder's way of imparting some life-changing and imperative information. "We need the designers to hit this deadline. I need a prototype."

"Yes, they are on track to deliver a working draft by the end of the year. I saw the wireframes this morning, but the VP wanted to review it before we showed it to you."

"Okay, the wireframes will work for my meeting with Investors this week. If you think it looks good, please just send it directly to me. We can skip the VP. I trust you."

Investors? What Investors? Who would invest in this fire truck set on fire? The New Hire had never heard the Founder, or anyone for that matter, ever mention Investors before. Were other people contributing to this failing enterprise?

The New Hire had to contend with chaos on multiple fronts. In addition to the unpredictability of the Founder, the Tech Czar frequently tried to undermine her. Annoyed that the New Hire no longer reported to her, the Tech Czar could not accept her as a peer. She would send emotionally charged messages to the Founder filled with emojis and personal insights.

Unsure what their real connection was, the New Hire treaded lightly. The Founder would often forward these confidential notes directly to the New Hire and Stepdaughter as an FYI. Another reason the New Hire never put anything incriminating in writing.

"Hey, did you read that email that just came in?" the New Hire would ask.

Shaking her head, the Stepdaughter would simply reply with an exaggerated eye roll. "She is so ridiculous. I can't even handle it."

Not only did the Tech Czar try to ingratiate herself with the Founder, but the Stepdaughter had long suspected she read any email sent through the company server. "Oh, you know we don't put anything in writing," glancing over to Happiness.

Taken slightly aback, the New Hire looked up, desperate for a more details. Happiness added, "Um, yeah. Texting is much safer."

The New Hire took note. No further explanation was necessary or forthcoming.

The New Hire was careful not to put anything even somewhat controversial in writing. Like any person making questionable choices, the Tech Czar probably justified this practice as protecting the greater good. At most major companies, it is implied the IT group can read any employee email, but only for cause. As ever the exemplary employee, the Tech Czar was just trying to be "proactive," obviously.

The Tech Czar's behavior toward the New Hire continued to deteriorate. Nothing bothered her more than being left out. Since the Founder loved to come on-site and hold confidential meetings in the middle of the theater, this was like a dagger in her heart. As part of her "proactivity" drive, the Tech Czar would find creative ways to still be part of the action. As no one sat in the theater area per se, it was still the gateway to the old wardrobe rooms and IT storage.

One of the Tech Czar's most loyal followers had set up the office infrastructure, from the telephone wiring to the placement of the server. Whenever the Founder was conducting his not-so-secret/secret gatherings in which the Tech Czar was not involved, her Senior Technology Specialist would appear walking across the large theater.

His cover story never seemed too believable. Theoretically, everyone was in the office for forty hours. Yet, for the few random hours a week the Founder would appear, Senior Technology needed to check the server in the furthermost corner of the office. Without fail, whatever the topic, he would saunter across the open floor, trying to catch a word or two.

After the third coincidence, the Founder looked up and yelled, "Hurry up!" This empty threat did not deter Senior Technology as he continued to walk in "accidentally" on future open-space meetings the Founder held.

Even though the New Hire did not trust the Tech Czar—or her team—she remained polite and would unhappily engage in mindless chatter whenever their paths crossed. Most mornings, entering through the large glass doors, she saw an empty pod where the Technology group sat.

How could they build a product without the staff committed to working the hours necessary to launching the Beta? A team frequently absent from their desks did not shout, "Ready when you are!" When the New Hire turned the corner, she could not help thinking how premeditated the Tech Czar's seat selection. An early misgiving confirmed.

As her apprehension grew, fate seemed to intervene. As the New Hire was usually the second person to arrive at the Startup, without fail, she would stop to talk to the Office Manager—the only other person present.

"Morning. How are you today?" she asked.

"Fine. How are you? We're the only two here. Per usual," the Office Manager replied.

"I guess folks like to keep their own hours."

"Something like that. Actually, I was thinking about what happens if you were to get here before me?"

"I suppose I'd just wait in the hallway. But don't worry. I can't imagine you would be too much later."

"True. Still, I was thinking I should give you a set of keys."

"Oh, really?"

"Yes, here, I already have them cut. Besides, you should have a set in case of emergency. Or if I'm on vacation. Or if you need to come in earlier than me. Or if I'm running late. Ha ha. Anyway, I don't want you to get locked out!"

"Thank you for thinking of me. That's kind."

"No problem. Here, let me show you. This key is for the visitor's entrance. This one is for the theater. And this one opens up everything else."

Everything else? Curious, the New Hire wondered what other doors that final key might open. Something, literally, to keep in her back pocket for now.

CHAPTER 6

POOR POOR PITIFUL ME

In her one-on-one interactions with the Founder, the New Hire found him convincing. Earnest. He had an overabundance of ideas, flowing through him with the force and inconsistency of a dripping faucet. He could not stay focused. Constantly spinning the second plate. He didn't base decisions on data; instead, preferring his gut. The Founder always made direct eye contact, just to ensure the other person was onboard, before changing his mind the next time he spoke.

Even though they made little progress toward finalizing the Mobile App as the end of the year approached, the Founder was determined to hire a third-party to build the Beta prototype. It was a clear departure from his earlier pronouncement to keep the Developers in-house. He assigned the Tech Czar the task of compiling bids.

The Founder noted, loudly and often, "No friends or family involved. I want a trustworthy agency to build this thing once and for all. Let's get the app up and running before the next summer. I want to release the Beta by May."

The Startup shut down operations over the last two weeks of December so the staff could enjoy the holidays. During this period, the Founder messaged the New Hire asking her to review the Tech Czar's proposal. Receiving an after-hours request while the offices were closed was completely on-brand for the Founder. He expected all employees to be on call just in case he had a game-changing idea.

In her initial scan of the Founder's email, the New Hire was puzzled, as the recommendation only included two agencies. One had a price tag of two hundred thousand and the other of five hundred thousand. The lack of choices and cost discrepancy were noteworthy. Most proposals come in threes: good, better, and best. Why did this recommendation only have a high and low bid? Suspicious, the New Hire was anxious to tackle her assignment. She did not want to wait until the offices reopened to reply to the Founder.

Research. Cross-referencing. Solving the case. All things the New Hire loved to do. She could spend hours reviewing documents. Her semi-photographic memory, keen eye for inconsistencies, and attention to detail helped. Her childhood dream was to become a detective. Not a real one. She wanted to be like the ones you saw on TV. Before, of course, the fictional ones became so gritty. She was the self-proclaimed Laura Holt, Maddie Hayes, or Dee Dee McCall of any corporate workplace.

Reviewing the cheaper company's profile online, the New Hire noticed something off almost instantaneously. The biggest client of Product Development Agency was the same prominent University the Tech Czar attended and frequently mentioned. It also was the same University where the majority of her gaggle of groupies had previously worked.

How unusual was it that Product Development Agency was bidding approximately half of the price of a more well-known and respected agency? The New Hire felt like she was watching a rerun of *Murder, She Wrote*, and not an especially good one. Whatever aging star received top billing that week was obviously the murderer.

The New Hire consulted her previous employer's most well-known product. She typed the secret formula into a search box: Person's Name + Company Name = Case Solved. Sure enough, the Tech Czar was listed as the sole owner of Product Development Agency.

Wasn't this too obvious? Even Jessica Fletcher had to contend with a few red herrings to throw viewers off the scent. Could the Tech Czar be so lazy as to not even attempt to cover her self-dealing tracks? She must be missing something.

The more the New Hire thought about it, she realized the Tech Czar's ego was too big for her not to leave her calling card. She hungered for attention, approval, and adulation. All things the New Hire loved to withhold from people who craved them most.

Convinced the Tech Czar was violating the Startup's ethics policy, even by the most liberal interpretation, the New Hire still proceeded carefully. Fearing the Tech Czar read all emails sent through the company server, she replied to the Founder.

Subject: RE: Recommendations

The proposals look good. I just have a few questions, so let me know when you have a moment to chat.

While she did not have definitive proof the Tech Czar still actively ran her former company, it was a pretty large omission not to disclose her association with the Agency she recommended for a substantial contract.

The New Hire called the Founder to lay out her case against the Tech Czar. Her role was not to judge but rather to present the facts. She would let the Founder draw his own conclusions. After exchanging hellos, she jumped in.

"I carefully reviewed both proposals. As you know, one is substantially cheaper than the other. Can I ask, what way are you leaning?"

Without hesitation, the Founder mentioned the significantly discounted company. "I like the first option. They seem to cover everything we need, no? I'm not sure what the real difference is in the details, but I do like the price."

His logic made sense. At the end of the day, both companies would be delivering a fully functional Mobile App. Why spend three hundred thousand dollars unnecessarily?

"So, did the Tech Czar happen to mention she had ties to the Product Development Agency?" the New Hire asked.

"No," the Founder firmly replied.

Trying to hedge, the New Hire continued, "I'm not sure if the material I found is still current, so please take everything with a grain of salt. Through my online research, I found the Tech Czar listed as the Agency owner. Again, I want to warn you the information I found could be outdated. Regardless, I am confident she either still owns or, at one time, owned this company."

The Founder took a moment. Through the shaky cell phone connection, the New Hire could hear his frustration and outrage.

"Thank you for your insights," he said. "You've done a great job. I really appreciate your thoroughness. Okay, I will take care of this. Thank you again. Also, I will not forget this either. I mean it."

In typical fashion, the Founder's response was to email the Tech Czar and blind copy the New Hire:

Subject: Proposals

I am traveling this week with my extended family for the holidays. I was not able to call earlier, as discussed, so we will have to wait until after the New Year to connect.

I reviewed both proposals very carefully and have the following commentary:

1. I researched the company you said was your first choice, and to my surprise, they only had testimonials from one really big client, your former employer. With all the money I am willing to spend, I want a company with mobile app building experience, not just media.
2. I was mildly perturbed to find your name listed as an owner in the process. I absolutely do not want this type of affiliation! We have had the friends and family discussion many times. As a nonnegotiable, I want an arm's length contract. This revelation in itself is enough to pass.
3. I am confused why we are not building a more sustainable app. I have mentioned this to you numerous times. The cost is the cost. As I have told you, also many times, this is my priority. My only priority! We should have already invested several million dollars into this endeavor. I will not have sticker shock if investing more is what it takes to get things done.
4. I expect you, as the Chief Information Officer, to recommend companies. I know you have

attended conferences and have years of experience and expertise. You can easily find alternative recommendations.

5. I must break this hierarchical issue with you. Also, we have discussed this many times. If you can't get over this, we will have to figure out how to proceed.

To that end, I would like to meet with you first thing on Tuesday after the break. My intent is not to be so harsh, but we both know you can do better. In the future, I do not want to have to take the time to research these things. Instead, I want to rely and depend on your good judgment. Please consider these points, and let's get a contract done when we return.

You know I love and care for you very much. This is business, though. I am losing my patience with some of your approaches—be prepared in January.

I wish you a very happy New Year. I want you to enjoy the rest of your vacation. Please do not call me. I will be unable to respond further until next week.

xoxo

The Founder's response should not have dumbfounded the New Hire, but somehow it did. What was the Founder's core message? Love? Fear? Loathing? All three or none of the above? Was this a work email?

The takeaway was clear: At any other company, the Tech Czar would have been fired on the spot. Post haste. Return to sender. *Alice Doesn't Live Here Anymore.* But not at this place of business.

Coming back from the holiday, the New Hire did not know what to expect. She should have foreseen the outcome but somehow hadn't.

The Tech Czar was already in damage control, not only playing the role of spin doctor but also whipping her allies into a frenzy.

"He was finally ready to pull the trigger. I recommended two agencies. Two options. Easy, right? To make the choice even easier, I included a group I previously worked with. I know these guys. They're great people. They even gave me a break on the price. I mean really nice, right? Stupid me as I really thought we could actually get this thing built. But ooohhh nooo! We can't do anything that makes sense. We're all set and then, for some unknown reason, he changes his mind. Again! He just changed his mind! That's it! We were all set. I know these guys. It would be so effortless to work with them. But oooohhh nooo. We can't do anything easy!" she bellowed to the VP and Head of Design just loud enough so the rest of the floor could hear her complain.

"Now, I have to go back to the drawing board. Again! He wants me to find three completely different companies again to bid on our app development. Can you believe that?"

The New Hire had to give the Tech Czar credit for getting ahead of the story. In his email, the Founder presented himself as the detective and discoverer of unethical deeds. To the New Hire, it seemed blatantly obvious she was the source of the exposé. Who else could it be? Did the Tech Czar honestly believe the Founder researched her proposal carefully and learned of her deception on his own?

The New Hire firmly believed that over time, people reveal their true selves. She had little desire to unveil the Tech Czar for who she knew her to be. She was happy to let the Tech Czar spin her narrative, even though she knew it was untrue.

By the end of the first week back in the office, and after much prodding from the Founder, the Tech Czar presented him with three additional choices.

Clearly, her time away from the office had been eventful. Not only did the Tech Czar spend hours compiling her fanciful tale about the agency selection process, but also Monster was back in tow. There was one slight difference, however. Monster was wearing a diaper. And not a cute one, either. Not the one with the Saturday Morning Cartoon characters. Nope, this looked like old-fashioned Depends, and before they redesigned them to look like underwear.

To make conversation, and maybe to cut what she perceived as tension, the New Hire inquired about Monster's status. "Oh my. Is she okay?"

"Oh, yeah. She will be. She has her period."

The New Hire didn't realize puppies could get periods. Sure, it made sense biologically, but she had never seen a diaper-wearing dog before. And certainly, she had never witnessed it before in a professional workplace setting, and obviously, she had never had a discussion about puppy periods with another human being before.

"Oh, I see," the New Hire replied, assuming the chat was over.

For unknown reasons, the Tech Czar continued describing Monster's predicament, "Yeah, because of the period, she'll need to be in a diaper around-the-clock for the next several days. It's really hard to find dog diapers in her size since she's already so big."

"Oh."

"What's especially annoying is changing the diaper. Whenever she pees or poops or even when it just gets too heavy, I have to change it. I am, like, constantly feeling it to see if she has gone."

"Hmm."

"Since we are going to get her spayed soon, the vet said it is better to let your puppy have its first menstruation cycle. If she has that first cycle, the vet said she would retain more of her personality."

More of her personality? The one where she pees and poops whenever and wherever she pleases?

That Golden Earring song popped into the New Hire's head. Yes, she was stepping into the "Twilight Zone."

"Anyway, this is our life for the next few days," the Tech Czar added.

The New Hire was speechless. When she asked if Monster was okay, the correct answer was, "Yep. She's fine." End of story. End of discussion. No other details were required or appreciated.

Did the Tech Czar really not know that even Betty White, a world-renowned pet lover, would not have wanted to hear about a dog's period? Why would someone share this story with someone they barely knew, let alone a coworker?

The New Hire shouldn't have been surprised, but yet somehow still was. This was the same person who aggressively spit onto the carpet by the food table—twice.

CHAPTER 7

YOU'VE GOT A FRIEND IN ME

Despite evidence to the contrary—no product, no customers, and no income—the team accelerated forward. With the new year came a renewed thrust from the Founder. The Chief Happiness Officer began opening requisitions for additional headcount. Feeling more empowered, the New Hire pushed for more individual accountability, especially from the Tech Czar and VP.

With a brand-new, nonaffiliated Mobile App Development Agency on board, the New Hire was able to put together a project plan and roadmap. As the number of deadlines increased, so did the meetings with the Founder. The New Hire was working more closely with the Stepdaughter to get things done.

The pair shared a bond. Sitting across from each other, they would frequently chat over the desks.

"Did you watch *The Handmaid's Tale*?" the Stepdaughter asked. "They just released a new episode last night. It was so, so, so good."

"Oh my god, yes! I think we now know if our credit cards stop working, we need to drop everything and head straight to Canada. Do not pass go, do not collect two hundred dollars! That's the mistake June and Moira made!" the New Hire replied.

"Totally. It's always the little things that mess you up."

The more time passed, the more the New Hire began to consider the Stepdaughter a friend. She liked having someone to confide in and maintain her sanity. They had similar world views and shared interests. Their banter was effortless.

"I'm so impressed you not only carry that Hydro Flask everywhere with you, but also use it," the New Hire said.

"You gotta stay hydrated, yo," the Stepdaughter replied.

"With water? Does coffee count?"

"Um, no. No, coffee does not count."

"Do you think my lack of water is why I'm always thirsty?"

"Oh man, I'm buying you a Hydro Flask today! You need to drink water!"

"You want me to drink a whole one of those things? Every day? Are you crazy? That seems like a lot of water."

"Dude, if you drink an entire Hydro, every day, for one month, I'll take you to IHOP."

"IHOP? Oooh. That is so tempting. Can we walk there?"

"Ha ha. Okay, but you have to legitimately drink the entire Hydro. I mean, I'm literally going to fill it for you and check to see you've finished the whole thing at the end of the day. Plus, you have to do it every day, including weekends, for an entire month. No cheating."

"No cheating? Ugh, you're really tying my hands here. So, if I drink the Hydro every day for a month, including weekends, you'll buy me lunch at IHOP and we can walk there?"

"Yep, that's right. And no cheating."

"Okay, I promise. Every day for a month, including weekends, and no cheating. It's a deal. Can I complain?"

"Nope."

* * *

With the Stepdaughter mainly focused on completing her PhD program, she would often come in midmorning and leave early to get to class. She, however, was happy to collaborate with the New Hire and push for action. They became a team—Lucy and Ethel. Mary and Rhoda. Good cop, bad cop. Cagney and Lacey. The New Hire owned the strategy and direction of the product, while the Stepdaughter pushed for execution and followed up with the laggards, when she wasn't studying, of course.

With the Mobile App Development Agency in place, the internal team became more focused. After months and months of stops and false starts, all the various components of building something were coming together to form a semi-functional prototype. Understanding the priorities, dependences and sequencing were crucial to ensuring success. In these stress-inducing times, the New Hire experienced firsthand how unqualified the other managers were.

Often, when given direction and a plan, people step up and shine. The VP, who the New Hire had once liked so much, was not this person. She was much more concerned with having power than contributing to the bottom line. Apparently, she missed the memo explaining she worked at a Startup. Everyone chips in. Leave your ego at the door.

Her interactions with the designers were interchangeable, one indistinguishable from the next. Reruns. The same episode without the special guest star. The subject matter might change, but the broad strokes and topics were identical. Whenever the New Hire observed her talking to her team, the conversations were all variations on the same theme.

"I saw the prototype mock-up that's being circulating. Why? I didn't approve the revisions. You shouldn't be sending anything around I haven't approved," the VP complained.

"I'm sorry about that, but I did send them to you for your approval. It was last week? The Founder had emailed me directly asking for the latest version. I sent you a follow-up note asking for your okay, but maybe you missed it? He asked a second time, so I sent him what I had. I apologize, but you did see them," the Lead Designer answered.

"Why's the Founder going directly to you? He knows I must approve everything! Well, regardless, I have changes for you."

"Sure, I'm happy to make any updates. The Founder said he liked what I sent, but I'm more than willing to incorporate your changes into the final too."

Likely a holdover from her corporate days, the VP measured her strength in headcount. Like a relic from a bygone generation, she was obsessed with building her empire and ensuring as many direct reports as possible. She would ask team members to pick up her dry cleaning, schedule personal appointments, or memorize her coffee order.

The New Hire struggled to get anything resembling a deliverable from the VP. Responsibilities inherently tied to her title, like a Go-to-Market Plan, Marketplace Research Trends, or a Marketing Risk Analysis, were mired in excuses. The VP was quick to pass the buck, which could explain her bizarre symbiotic relationship with the Tech Czar.

The interactions between the VP and Tech Czar were painful to watch. The cringe-worthy nicknames the New Hire overheard in the interview were neither a fluke nor an inside joke. While the duo went out of their way to describe each other in an overly complimentary way, they were also quick to throw the other under the bus.

They supported the other's ideas with flattery until any sort of probing question like, "How will that work?" was asked. Quickly, each would independently disavow any responsibility toward not only each other, but also toward whatever work was being done.

Calling one of his impromptu theater meetings, the Founder gathered all his leaders: the Tech Czar, the VP, Happiness, the Stepdaughter, and the New Hire. He announced his new purpose: hit the Agency's deadlines to release the Beta on time.

The Founder started: "What do we need to make this happen? This is our number-one priority. I want all-hands-on-deck. Are there any risks?"

The request seemed reasonable, as the Founder had signed a half-million-dollar contract with the Agency to build the prototype and release the Beta. The VP declared: "Yes. We need to fire the Lead Designer. She's insubordinate. If we don't get rid of her, I don't see how we can effectively work with the Agency."

The New Hire was stunned. If there was one person on staff who actually had done work to move the project forward, it was the Lead Designer. She put together the initial mock-up, laid out the wireframes, and captured all the requirements necessary for the Development team to create the Mobile App infrastructure.

The New Hire did not want to show too much emotion, but she was confused, angry, and upset. She considered the Lead Designer an ally. One of the few people at work the New Hire could depend on to execute. She was the most valuable employee the Startup had.

Experience taught the New Hire to hold her cards tight. While she believed in speaking her mind, she also knew how to maximize her influence. By not immediately reacting, she had a chance to read the room and take a more measured approach. At work, at least, the New Hire could be patient, a personality trait that did not come naturally to her. By displaying restraint, she was more efficient and, ultimately, more effective.

On the inside, the New Hire mentally listed out ten reasons why the Lead Designer should stay and the VP should go, culminating with this moment. On the outside, she took a deep breath. The Lead Designer's contributions were painfully obvious, but the Founder, who often called staff by the wrong name, might not realize her true value. The New Hire closed her eyes briefly, hoping to transmit this message telepathically. Simply suggesting the firing of someone so crucial to delivering the launched product when they were so close to breaking through the stalemate proved to the New Hire that the VP was motivated by ego, not performance.

The Founder looked at the VP with a smirk. He removed his glasses and directly addressed her. "Now, I know you like a certain hierarchy, like your friend over there [pointing to the Tech Czar], but from what I can tell, the Lead Designer is the one person who's gotten us this far. Why do you think we should fire her?"

Digging in her heels, the VP explained: "She doesn't follow protocol and has an attitude problem. Here is a perfect example: The designs currently circulating haven't been approved by me."

Trying not to sigh out loud, the New Hire caught the Stepdaughter's glance, who discreetly shook her head. The New Hire knew they were on the same page. They both had seen multiple emails from the Lead Designer asking for the VP's feedback. After a week of not getting any input, the Lead Designer went ahead and put together a mock-up, which was required for the Agency to begin its work.

Also sensing the Founder was aligned, the Stepdaughter held back from saying anything. Taking a short break, the Founder addressed the VP again. "Well, I don't know what to say. In my book, she's produced all the designs so far. She stays."

Annoyed, the VP crossed her arms and slid back in her chair.

Once the Founder ended the meeting, the VP asked if she could speak to him privately. Even though he was crystal clear, both the Stepdaughter and New Hire appreciated the VP would never let this, or anything, go without a fight.

While the rest of the team headed back into the main area, she began campaigning and participating in her favorite pastime: trying to reverse all the Founder's previously made decisions. Usually, she had moderate success convincing him to change direction. This time, the VP failed.

As the New Hire trailed behind Happiness and the Stepdaughter, she took notice again how close they were. Knowing where all the bodies were buried, Happiness would frequently whisper with the Stepdaughter, presumably about other colleagues. The New Hire would only hear the tail end of these confidential conversations: "Well, you know what I think about that one! Um, yeah."

During the meeting, the New Hire was a little surprised Happiness did not offer any defense of the Lead Designer. Maybe she too was waiting for the Founder to weigh in, but she did run employee relations. The New Hire thought she must shutdown the VP because her request was to fire someone for not bending to her every whim. But the New Hire had already concluded that Happiness was not necessarily an exemplary employee, especially for someone who worked in human resources. Who censors the censor?

Not only did Happiness love to gossip about others, frequently, but also she often signed her emails, "Have a blessed day!" While not offended, the New Hire found it odd and slightly off-putting. Signing a personal note with your religious beliefs was perfectly fine, but seeing it on company-wide memos was not really appropriate. Maybe the New Hire was more offended that Happiness often tried to dampen payment delays with her overt messages of gratitude.

> **Subject: Payroll Update**
>
> Please be advised the payroll scheduled for Monday will now be processed on Wednesday or Thursday. At such time, payments will be deposited into your accounts. Thank you for your patience, and my apologies.
>
> Have a blessed week!

Regardless of these quirks, the New Hire did develop a deeper friendship with Happiness as she grew closer to the Stepdaughter. While the New Hire wasn't entirely sure she could trust Happiness, she liked her. Happiness was funny, direct, and unpredictable—but in a good way.

"Stop me if I have complained about this before. My dumb ex is now insisting the kids fly back to South Carolina for their March break. They just visited him in December for Christmas. I was like, 'Um, you gonna pay for that?'" Happiness stated emphatically.

"Eek. Do you think he's serious?" the New Hire asked.

"Hell no! It's just a ploy. He knows I am looking to buy some property in Tennessee, near my family."

"Tennessee! Would you move?"

"Girl, you think I'm gonna work here forever?"

"Ha ha. No, I do not!"

"Trust me, this gig is just a stopover. I'm thinking about a couple of different things. When the kids finish high school in a few years, yeah, definitely, I would move back home."

"When you say Tennessee, do you mean near Memphis or Nashville? Or are you talking about the countryside?"

"Country all the way, baby! I've been running a Talent Consulting Firm on the side for several years. We do executive recruiting. If we can get a few more evergreen clients, I could do it. I could move."

"Oh, interesting. Is that how you know the Founder?"

"No, no. I do the recruiting after-hours and only for private clients. I came in and interviewed for this role just like you. I wanted to put Startup experience on my resume."

"Ha ha. Funny, me too."

"Careful what you wish for, right?"

"Ha ha. Right. You just might get it."

The New Hire did have a momentary pause when Happiness mentioned her side recruiting gig. Didn't the Chief Happiness Officer work at the Startup full time? Plenty of people have side hustles, but they don't usually announce it—especially when they run Human Resources.

Even though the New Hire preferred keeping her lunchtime free to either go for a walk in the neighborhood or explore the building, she usually could be tempted to share a meal with the Stepdaughter and Happiness. She did not necessarily go out of her way to suggest grabbing lunch, but rarely turned down an invitation.

The crew especially enjoyed a local pirate-themed dive bar that made incredible salads. Usually, Happiness would initiate plans in the morning,

"I didn't feel like making lunch today. Where should we go?"

The Stepdaughter would sometimes suggest a Filipino place within a ten-minute walk. "If we want to head on a little adventure, we can get chicken adobo."

Not the New Hire's favorite, she depended on the closeness of the pirate bar to outweigh any momentary dietary preferences. As the morning approached 11:45, Happiness would more often than not say, "I'm starving. Let's just go up the street to the pirate bar."

* * *

The Founder grew restless with the pace of progress. He lived in the moment, and he wanted to build his Mobile App—now. Capitalizing on the Founder's impatience, the Tech Czar pushed an Open Beta release by August. While in principle the New Hire agreed with the timeline, from a financial point of view, launching to the public made little sense.

Never sure what exactly motivated the Founder, the New Hire put together another analysis. She followed-up with her recommendations with an email.

LAUNCH DECISION

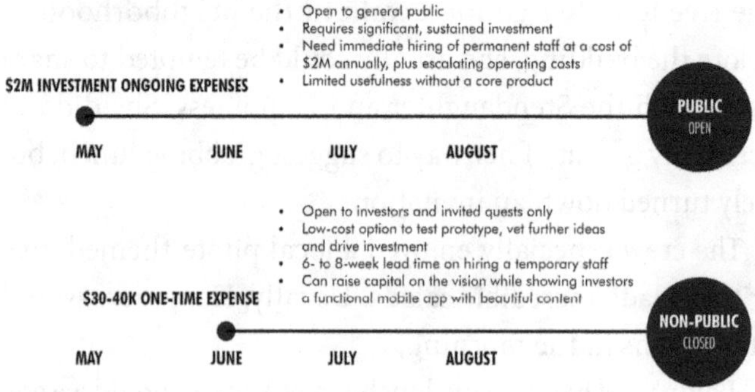

Subject: Launch Considerations

I put together a quick overview of where we are and some factors to consider for our launch. Weighing the risks and rewards of both options, I think we should plan for a non-public release instead of a public one. By having a Closed launch, development can continue to either refine ideas further or change direction within the existing infrastructure. We can use the prototype to raise funds with Investors and pursue more economically viable ideas.

Also, a more measured approach gives us a chance to evaluate our strategy to streamline the product and develop a core idea while still defining the North Star for the company.

Thoughts?

Within an hour, the Founder replied.

Subject: RE: Launch Considerations

K. Do it.

With direction from the Founder, the New Hire decided it was the time to push the Tech Czar. By any objective definition, her role in the Startup was to make technology tradeoffs. Moving ahead with a Closed Beta launch meant moving from theoretical to practical. How could they set up the backend workings of the Mobile App that was flexible enough to pivot in the future? The Tech Czar had an allergy to taking a point of view.

Using the Agency as coverage, the New Hire pressed the Tech Czar for answers, as her inability to decide would now cause delays, which, in turn, would cost money. Listing a series of tasks—analytics, linking and search engine optimization strategy, features, policy standards—the New Hire sent out an invitation and included the Stepdaughter.

Privately, the New Hire complained, "Why is this so hard? All she has to do is pick a path for the Beta. We can always change track later."

"I know. She's lazy and doesn't want to do any work," the Stepdaughter replied.

Setting a meeting at 2:00 p.m. on a Thursday could be a crapshoot. The Tech Czar loved to take extended lunches with her team at the local Mexican restaurant known for its bottomless margarita pitcher. Similar to the well-known Jimmy Buffet song, they were definitely searching for their lost shaker of salt.

Funnily, the Tech Czar had a massive tell whenever she took advantage of the café's lunchtime special. While she usually wore a uniform of crisp, button-down shirts deeply tucked into her pants, after these mostly liquid affairs, the Tech Czar's shirt would be untucked. Her hair, usually in the tightest of ponytails, would also be out of place. She looked disheveled.

Sending a quick text to push the meeting by an hour, the New Hire and the Stepdaughter waited in the front meeting room for the Tech Czar to arrive.

Announcing her arrival, she yelled out, "Oh, hi guys. Sorry I'm late." Clearly overserved, the Tech Czar continued with the meeting. "So, what are we discussing?"

Not only had the New Hire sent her several emails throughout the week asking about the status of the running list of to-dos, but also she included a meeting agenda.

"Let's start with the agenda I sent. Maybe you can update us on where everything is?"

"Ah, yes. Update on where everything is. I mean, you're a real detective, aren't you? You just know everything, don't you? You just need to know everything. You keep harassing me about the list. Don't you?" The Tech Czar rebutted.

Detective? Could it be that after several months, the Tech Czar finally figured out the New Hire uncovered her ethical violations? Yes, the Tech Czar was slightly drunk, but it was a strange non sequitur, even for her.

Intrigued but trying to stay on track, the New Hire continued, "Well, I think the questions are pretty straightforward. We just need to know where everything is, what still needs to be done, and how we make sure we are hitting all our deadlines. What can we do to help you?"

The Tech Czar would not let it go, though. Maybe someone on her team figured it out? The New Hire was the reason the Founder refused to use her Product Development Agency, probably costing her hundreds of thousands of dollars in secret revenue. The hostility had been brewing. The New Hire preferred to stay focused on their meeting objectives and planned to follow up separately with the Tech Czar individually. The Tech Czar, however, had a different idea.

"You know everything anyway. Why don't you tell me what the status is?"

Taking a moment to respond, the New Hire was genuinely bewildered. She felt they blew past the "Can We Still Be Friends" stage, and like the song, things just could not go on like before.

The New Hire was ready to defend her position if that was what the Tech Czar wanted, but it seemed like a terrible hill to die on. The Stepdaughter interrupted.

"No! Absolutely not. I will not have you come in here late when you've had several cocktails and berate her! No! Not happening! We're not having this discussion today. When you are ready to have an adult conversation, you can come and apologize. After you apologize, we'll be happy to chat. We're leaving."

The Stepdaughter grabbed her notebook, laptop, and Hydro Flask. She stormed out. Astonished at what had just occurred, the New Hire trailed quickly behind.

Hurrying her pace to catch up with the Stepdaughter, the New Hire smiled and said, "That was so fantastic. I cannot believe you did that!"

The Stepdaughter, still annoyed by the Tech Czar, simply replied, "No way. There is no way I will allow that to happen. She can't talk to you that way!"

CHAPTER 8

BRILLIANT DISGUISE

As the whole team was pushing ahead with plans to launch the Beta prototype, the Founder decided it, of course, was the perfect time to get into cryptocurrencies. A risky venture, shrouded somewhat in mystery, with no tangible by-product and questionable outcomes? Check, check, and check. A forgone conclusion. A decentralized, digital currency was tailor-made for a startup that had a construction site but no visible sign of any construction workers.

On Monday morning, the Crypto King appeared. He arrived around 10:00 and walked through the U-shaped office to take a seat in the same row as the New Hire. No introductions. No explanations.

Confused, the New Hire stared at the Stepdaughter with a blank expression on her face, who briefly smiled before averting her eyes to avoid laughing.

Grabbing her phone, the New Hire discreetly texted the Stepdaughter.

Um.

Yep. This is happening.

What you talkin' 'bout, Willis?

Ha. Didn't I tell you? We are a cryptocurrency company now!

That makes zero sense. Also, I missed one day in the office!

This is what happens when you take a day off. Crypto is the next big thing. Did you not know that?

And how will this help us release the Mobile App?

Oh, it is mission critical. Obvi.

Oy with the poodles already.

Don't worry. Nothing will be okay.

After reading her final text, the New Hire looked up at the Stepdaughter. She rolled her eyes and shook her head in disbelief.

Taking a deep, cleansing breath, the New Hire took the initiative to introduce herself to the Startup's latest employee.

"Hi there. Welcome to the team."

"Hi."

"So, I understand you'll be working on cryptocurrencies?"

"Yep."

"Great. Sounds like an interesting and growing field."

"Yep."

"I guess you'll be figuring out how it fits into our future plans?"

"Yep."

Sensing the futility of continuing, the New Hire bailed on the conversation. "Well, nice to meet you. Welcome again."

The Crypto King barely spoke to her again. The New Hire was surprised, as people who are passionate about somewhat moderately fringe topics usually cannot wait to prophesize and convert the masses. To make matters equally awkward, they technically sat next to each other.

The New Hire was especially perplexed to see the Crypto King in person. Considering these invisible currencies were invented for, and by, a purely digitally native audience, you might assume the Founder would have employed someone born after 1988. To the New Hire, the Crypto King materialized from nothing, from nowhere. A sudden flash in the night sky that stays within view longer than it should. Not wanting to be presumptive, but to her, this guy did not necessarily scream "I work in emerging technologies" for a living.

If the Crypto King had indeed reinvented himself later in life, it was not evident by his appearance. He wore old, faded jeans that not only lacked any form but also were too light for modern fashions. Paired with a well-worn plaid, flannel, button-down shirt, Crypto's style could be considered a failed attempt at grunge. And thirty years too late.

Nothing about his dress indicated an interest in cutting edge. Then, less than fourteen days into his new role, the Crypto King booked a three-week fishing vacation. The Founder paid him for the time off. By the start of his third month, and what most people would consider the end of a ninety-day probationary period, Crypto delivered his long-awaited White Paper.

Covering the current position of cryptocurrency in the United States, the New Hire was eager to read his analysis. Skimming the research Crypto compiled, she noticed multiple footnote citations but no bibliography backing up his findings. *Hmm. Maybe he forgot to include the final page?* Something else struck the New Hire as odd. She saw an excessive amount of u's, as in the letter. Stranger still, these u's found their way into several words (favourite, colour, rumour), many would consider the British spelling.

Eager to downplay her concerns, the New Hire waited until Crypto went to lunch. Between the monitors, she caught Happiness's attention.

"Hey, do you have a copy of his resume?" nodding in the general direction of the Crypto King's area. "I'm reading through his findings, and I'm a little curious about his background."

"Sure. Give me a few minutes, and I'll email it to you."

Opening the file, the New Hire reviewed it carefully. *Okay, no British schooling.* Reading more closely, she stumbled over his education. *MBA? That guy?* He didn't speak like other MBAs she knew. In fact, he didn't speak.

Out of sheer curiosity, the New Hire typed the university name into her favorite Search Engine (and previous employer). Without clicking onto a single article, the recurring phrase popping up across her screen was Diploma Mill. The result from the Better Business Bureau read: "web-only institution that offered illegitimate degrees including online certificate programs, general life-experience degrees, and doctorates in religion." *No more calls. We have a winner!*

The New Hire's favorite highlight: Not only did the Crypto King pay for a bachelor's degree from this fake university but also sprung for the deluxe package, which included a master's degree. Allegedly. Armed with these newly discovered facts, the New Hire took a closer look at the White Paper. *Fake degree, fake paper? Could explain the lack of proper citations and strange spellings.* Returning to her favorite pastime researching, the New Hire typed the first paragraph into the search bar.

"Déjà Vu." Like the song, she had been there before, and she did know just what to do.

The New Hire presented her case to the Founder. Straightforward and direct.

"So, I was reading the White Paper, and something didn't seem right. It was well-researched, but all the citations were missing. Maybe 'missing' is not the right word. I think the right word is 'erased.'"

"I'm listening. Go on."

"Again, I don't know for sure, but when I copied the first paragraph into a search box, I found the entire White Paper, published by a British Blockchain Company. This is quite serious as it could leave us completely exposed, especially if we are sending White Paper to would-be Investors. Simply put, this is fraud."

Happiness was looped in and correctly felt the team needed more proof. The New Hire agreed, as stealing another person's work was a pretty heavy accusation. The Startup had to prove the Crypto King searched for the British Blockchain Company's White Paper and downloaded it onto his work laptop.

Since Happiness, the Stepdaughter, and the New Hire believed the Tech Czar was already reading emails, this was a made-to-order task. The plan: send a company-wide message announcing random laptop security checks during the week. The next day, Senior Technology Specialist came around the office with a rolling cart. He made one stop: next to the Crypto King's desk.

Senior Technology said, "Hi there. Did you see the email that went around regarding laptop security checks? Well, you guessed it! Your laptop was randomly selected. Can I grab it for the next hour?"

The unsuspecting Crypto King thought nothing of this highly unusual request. "Sure." He grabbed his wallet and popped out for a coffee.

His complete lack of suspicion made one thing abundantly clear to the New Hire. Crypto certainly did not attend university, let alone earn an MBA.

Senior Technology transferred the Crypto King's search and download history onto a thumb drive, and he presented it to Happiness. Gathering the New Hire and Stepdaughter, the trio drove over to the Shared Workspace Solutions headquarters to present their findings.

Happiness led the discussion: "We pulled his internet history from his entire tenure here. From June 14 to 16, he searched for the following terms: 'cryptocurrency white papers' and 'the future of cryptocurrency.' On June 16, he downloaded a previously published White Paper discussing the merits of the new currency in the United Kingdom. We can see he opened it in Word and edited the document."

Ready to stand up and head back to the other offices, the New Hire felt this was an open-and-shut case, undeniable proof the Crypto King committed plagiarism.

Whoomp, there it is. QED. Thus, it is proven. Game over.

The Founder, however, was hesitant to fire the Crypto King. "So, I mean, really, how bad is this?"

Incredulous, Happiness responded without pulling any punches.

"Really bad. This isn't a negotiation. He plagiarized another company's work. We need to pull his entire email history. If he sent this to a prospective Investor, he's falsely represented us. That's serious and could have other legal ramifications."

After a week of insistence from Happiness, the Stepdaughter, and the New Hire, the Founder finally terminated Crypto's contract but paid him for the days he worked and the ones he did not. The Crypto King vanished from the Startup with the morning sun, collecting a tidy sum including reimbursement for his three-week holiday.

The New Hire couldn't believe the Founder's failure to act. First self-dealing and now plagiarism. Perhaps even more unbelievable was his next proclamation. Deciding the mistake with the Crypto King was a fluke, the Founder declared: "We should start a News Department to complement the Mobile App Division."

Dazed, the New Hire paused and looked at the Founder. *How do you square that circle? How would starting a News Department help with the release of the Mobile App? Regardless of the tenuous connection, how could he justify hiring more people?* Another false start.

The Founder continued, "I think we should look to the future. There's a real gap in the marketplace. We need a News Department to speak to Gen Z. I can hire a few freelance

Investigative Reporters to spec out some stories with a distinct voice. From a Gen Z point of view. Let's start creating our own content. In the long run, it will be more cost-effective than just curating it. I want to get this off the ground in the next week or so."

"Oh, um, okay. Do you think now is really the time to ramp a new team? A new product? We're finally getting traction with the Mobile App. We have a realistic timeline for delivery and a plan to soft launch within the next two months. Don't you think this might distract people?" the New Hire rebutted.

"Not at all. We can parallel path it. I'm confident we are on track with the App, so now is the time to diversify. It'll be a wholly different department working on News. I just feel like the marketplace is yearning to hear from this generation. There's a real opportunity to own the space."

Following the same instinct that decided it was time to invest in cryptocurrencies, for the Founder, now was the exact time to invest in a News Department. Within a week, he had selected six journalists. Remit: Create content for a nonexistent website. Website: Coming soon!

As promised, the News Department quickly slotted into any available open space on the seventh floor, filling it with excitement and buzz previously nonexistent. In many ways, the New Hire was jealous. She admired the drive, energy, and ambition of the reporters. Their mission was to create content and break the rules. They were not yet jaded by the problems of the Startup. The ambiguity. The anxiety. The instability.

At her former position at the Search Engine, uncertainty was a fact of life. Hirings. Firings. Change was the only constant. In that environment, stress could often run high. Information became a commodity. People who had this capital wanted to spend it. The strategic move was to save for a rainy day. But like any drought-stricken forest desperate for relief, the most likely scenario was a tinder fire. The New Hire thrived in these situations. The commodity brokers sought her out: She seemed empathic. She seemed trustworthy. She seemed in the know.

When playing in these high-stakes espionage games, one must learn how to keep the secrets of others. Those who did not master that trick would flame out rather quickly, wasting any advantage. The New Hire was an expert at flying close to that light with only the occasional scarring. The type that faded over time rather than the kind that left a permanent reminder. Usually. This trick had a limited shelf-life.

* * *

Even though the workload was steady, the New Hire still had a general feeling of dread. She had been at the Startup for nine months. She managed to keep her panic levels at bay, but it was time to reflect. Step back. The New Hire needed to separate facts from conjectures. She wanted to get a handle on the situation but feared her judgment was starting to become unreliable. Mentally, she made a list:

Fact: The team was building a product.

Fact: Cash flow was an issue, but she was not sure how much of an issue.

Fact: The Founder still wanted to bring on additional staff.

Fact: There was too much overhead.

Fact: The business had no revenue coming in, at least not from the Startup team's efforts.

Fact: The Founder made all decisions.

While there were lots of stops and starts, the New Hire, in good faith, could say the team had produced wireframes, outlining the basic functionality and purpose. They had painstakingly put together the technical requirements and worked closely with the Mobile App Development Company; a Beta version was imminent. The Go-to-Market Strategy, or, for that matter, the need or desire of the marketplace, was unclear. None of these typical red flags stopped the Founder. He had an ever-changing vision, and he wanted to release it to the general public.

The Founder loved to gather the New Hire, Happiness, and the Stepdaughter for answers regarding delays. These meetings had a heavy whiff of irony. The Founder spent a year-and-a-half, not to mention millions of dollars, surrounding himself with all the wrong people and then wondered aloud what was taking so long.

The New Hire suspected the Founder understood the limitations of his leaders: The Tech Czar did not know how to build a Mobile App, and the VP did not know how to drive or run Marketing.

What could go wrong?

One of the Founder's favorite bluffs was to threaten the livelihood of his Executive staff. Calling the Stepdaughter, Happiness, and the New Hire to his Ivory Towers, he announced he wanted to fire the VP. The New Hire knew not to get excited by this empty promise. She felt that if the Tech Czar had remained, so would the VP.

Sure, the VP was terrible at her job, paralyzed by her desire for power, unable to put the project first, and reluctant to make decisions, but she had a strange hold over the Founder. Recalling a similar speech he gave threatening to fire the Tech Czar after her conflict-of-interest fiasco, the New Hire listened patiently.

"She has to go. I think I really mean it this time. She's way too territorial. She holds up the process, and it's not what the Startup needs to move forward."

"You know how I feel," the New Hire added.

"I agree. She has to go. She's toxic to the rest of the team. What's the risk of getting rid of her?" the Stepdaughter said, echoing the many conversations she'd had with the New Hire on the subject.

Maybe the Tech Czar and the VP didn't so much cast a spell over the Founder, but perhaps he felt a certain loyalty to them. His reasonings were opaque to the New Hire. As with everything related to the Founder, she felt nothing could last forever. For now, at least, the two had managed to find a small loophole and escape their inevitable fate.

The New Hire took some small delight that the VP's future seemingly lay in the Executive leadership committee's hands. She appreciated the irony of how the VP tried to get the Lead Designer fired, but now it was her turn to stand for judgment. The New Hire took a moment to reflect. Despite his proclamation to the contrary, she guessed the Founder had no real intention of firing her. Even though the New Hire thought the VP was a morally bankrupt person, she did not want to see her lose her livelihood.

Happiness began: "I can draw up the paperwork today. The VP is poisonous to the other staff and doesn't pull her weight. We should get rid of her."

The Founder looked confounded and distressed.

Happiness understood he was not emotionally prepared to fire the VP. Whenever she pushed him too hard, the Founder was quick to threaten her with the same final fate, reminding her she too was dispensable. This did not deter Happiness. She enjoyed pushing his boundaries while calling his bluff.

The New Hire saw a different opening. "We could just demote her. Keep her on staff but remove all of her direct reports."

The Founder looked like a Cheshire Cat with his upper lip curled up ever so slightly. Addressing the New Hire directly, he said, "You would like that, wouldn't you?"

Seeing her Solomonian solution had wings, the New Hire wanted to give it a chance to fly. Responding, she said, "Look, Design can report to me. If we are serious about soft-launching in August, it's the only way forward. Otherwise, she'll continue to be a blocker. Plus, maybe if we make it uncomfortable enough, she'll leave on her own accord."

The Founder had little wiggle room. He took another minute to think about the New Hire's proposal and agreed. Since the VP had a nasty habit of talking the Founder out of decisions he made, the New Hire said, "You should send the VP a note now, informing her of the staffing change."

Happiness was also eager to see the VP declawed and offered to draft a note as they sat around the small round table. She quickly typed a memo that started with the words: "Effective immediately."

The New Hire would not be satisfied until the Founder sent the email.

Happiness drafted the letter and read it back to the others. The New Hire kept eye contact with the Founder until she heard him say the magic words: "Send it."

Feeling a small victory was at hand, the New Hire reflected. What had she really gained? She understood that instead of following through with his threats, the

Founder preferred to hold power over employee's heads. He loved to keep them on short leashes and pleading for their jobs.

The team was still driving cost, not profit. Since the product had not launched yet, all the New Hire's work was theoretical. Perhaps it would pay off eventually. Or maybe not.

And all the progress to date was not cheap. Between salaries for necessary (and unnecessary) staff, Tech Czar-purchased future-state tools, and at least three floors of office space (that she knew of), the New Hire estimated the Founder was splaying out at least one million dollars per month. By her calculations, he had already invested twenty million into the business.

The Founder continued paying salaries. Mostly. The New Hire heard rumors that he was selectively paying people, like a perverse version of Russian Roulette. The Founder would spin the dial and decide who had earned their keep that payment cycle, based on what he perceived their value to the business was. His habit of fudging the payment delivery date continued too. The delays were getting longer.

Subject: Payroll

All wires went out. Unfortunately, I had to attend a funeral this morning and, as a direct result, missed the wire cut off time. You will see the money in your accounts by 11:00 a.m. tomorrow. If you would like a confirmation of the transaction, please let me know, and I can send it over to you first thing in the morning.

Subject: Apologies

Due to a clerical mistake, the payroll just transferred now. Unfortunately, wires will not be available in your accounts until next Tuesday. I apologize for this unforeseen error. Thank you kindly for your patience.

Subject: Delay

My apologies. Payroll has not been processed. While I take full responsibility for the delay, please note that while trying to meet the deadline, the ever-increasing banking policies unexpectedly prevented us from withdrawing funds. We had tried to schedule this to happen before a certain date. Obviously, when we have our regular payroll system in place, these issues will become transparent. Unfortunately, this is our cross to bear. Fortunately, we are fast-approaching a late-phase! Again, I apologize for any inconvenience or frustration this may have caused you. Very best regards and thank you.

Subject: Update

Quick update: I had targeted today as our payroll date. Just so you know, I expect to get this done over the weekend and not today. For your information, the signor who I need is not available until that time. You should see the wires on Monday late afternoon or by Tuesday EOD.

The New Hire learned an assortment of interesting tidbits. The Founder frequently attended funerals, which prevented him from making payroll. He had several mystery health issues (miraculously, these ailments would self-heal without any noticeable changes to his physical appearance). And banks were closed on Jewish holidays, and not the ones she, or anyone else, had heard of—these were different ones. The unexplained and increasingly frequent hiccups caused the Founder much inconvenience and also prevented him from paying the staff. Whenever wages were late or missing, he would go incognito for days at a time. As soon as the money hit the bank accounts, abracadabra, the Founder would reemerge, either through email or at the Startup's offices.

With the rate of missed paychecks increasing, the creative-fiction apologies were no longer including the occasional cash bonus. Missing the scheduled deadline by a week or two did not seem so bad when the sorry came with a green bouquet of dollars. Within a two-month period, the New Hire received an extra six thousand dollars. When the incentives slowed, so did her patience.

CHAPTER 9

WATCHING THE DETECTIVES

So much of life at the Startup was good on paper. An innovative idea. A large staff. An expensive external Agency. A hiring surge. Keeping up appearances. Theoretical. *But where did all the snacks go?*

Once plentiful, the free food table now looked like a final sale rack on Christmas Eve at a discount retailer. Instead of an assortment of healthy choices and guilty pleasures, a solitary dish of individually wrapped breath mints occupied the middle of the table, taunting the staff. The mints were a sad reminder of what was.

Not far behind the food was the water. Empty five-gallon bottles lined the area beneath the bar. Eventually, the Office Manager bought in a large water-filtration pitcher from home. Employees would have to take turns refilling it throughout the day. With drinkable water in short supply, the Startup also entered a money drought. Payment delays were now gaps. Occasional cash mirages would fool the staff into believing the issues were in the past.

Employee morale was at an all-time low, for most. The News Department, however, seemed blissfully unaware. The New Hire always thought of The Beatles' song, "Across the Universe," when she walked by their desks. She could not stop hearing the well-known chorus on auto play in her head.

The Reporters happily continued to pitch story ideas, oblivious to the current pay disruption.

"We could do something trendy. Environment? Social justice? Equality? What about a John Oliver-esque exposé?" the Editor-in-Chief would say.

"That could work. Or we could do something local," one of the Reporters piped in.

"That's good too. I wonder if we should start hyper-local while we're establishing our street creed. Maybe it could be a real differential? Something to make us stick out?"

"True. True. Whatcha thinking?"

"In Hollywood, what is there? Celebrity? Sex? Food? Crime?"

"Yes, exactly. That's it. Celebrity, sex, food, and crime. In that order!"

"Or better yet, all four together!"

The New Hire kind of enjoyed hearing the flow of ideas on the floor. That passion was missing from the rest of the team. The News Department scoured the internet for inspiration. During momentary fits of delusion, the New Hire thought their content could turn into something. A disorganized and chaotic bullpen. Energy. Enthusiasm. Breaking news. She vacillated between admiring their resolve and hating their naivety. Should she say something? Or give them a fighting chance before it was too late?

After catching up once again on payroll, the Founder summoned the New Hire, Happiness, and Stepdaughter to his Shared Workspace Solutions headquarters.

"I know it has been an extended period where y'all didn't get paid this time, but I had to rearrange a few things to find some additional funds. Listen, we knew this early summer period was going to be a struggle, but I am confident we're on the other side now," he said, trying to convey confidence.

We knew this summer period was going to be a struggle? We did? The New Hire remained quiet.

Happiness chimed in, expressing concern, "I'll be honest. This is a bad look. I'm warning you, people will not stand for this. Employees are either going to leave or stop showing up."

"We're turning the corner. I'm just asking for a little patience. I don't think it's that unreasonable. I've been enormously generous with salaries and benefits. Folks have to understand that, and that's why I pay you. We're on the verge of the Beta. While it was definitely a little sticky, that's behind us. We're moving forward. I'm going to assume you'll handle the communication piece?" the Founder replied, slightly annoyed.

Realizing the apologetic emails would continue, along with likely larger payment gaps, the New Hire needed a plan. Despite the Founder's assurances, she felt getting paid with a regular occurrence would be a problem. As she weighed risks and rewards, many questions still remained unanswered.

By design, the Founder created his own version of the New Jersey suburb where Tony, Carmela, and Cousin Christopher lived. A Soprano—minus the killing, of course. His mentality was the same as the mafia boss. Family. Loyalty. Don't ask. Don't tell. Employees were required to kiss the ring as the Founder dangled just enough cheese to trap his staff. This particular brand of cheddar was the promise of unpaid wages plus bonuses. He caught up before. Why couldn't he do it again? To get out, an employee would have to build a better mousetrap.

The New Hire had one nagging thought in the back of her head: What financial crimes was the Founder committing? Where did the Startup's money come from? Why were they spending exorbitant amounts of money on unnecessary people, places, and things—constantly? What was happening with the construction? Were there really any outside Investors?

The unofficial motto of the office could have been: All Hail the Founder! But was he the only one making decisions? From what the New Hire observed, other key players had spheres of influence but ultimately seemed limited in what they could accomplish. Sooner or later, the Founder would threaten them with banishment from his kingdom but never followed through.

Since the team was on track to release the Beta in August, the New Hire had temporarily wounded the VP with the demotion, but she still had the ear of the Founder. And so did the Tech Czar. The blows were not fatal. Surely, they would resurrect, perhaps stronger once they realized there were insignificant consequences for their actions. For now, they were slightly weaker; however, both were still forces to overcome. It was like some terrible, never-ending video game with an infinite scroll feature. Unlike most first-player shoot 'em-ups, scoring the most points did not seem to be the way to win.

The Startup was feeling more like Alcatraz than a place of employment. The cracks were becoming fault lines. The New Hire evaluated her options, and one thing was clear: She needed an exit strategy.

When payroll had fallen behind the first time, the New Hire updated her resume. She put out feelers, but without a launched product or Beta prototype, selling her experience to prospective employers was tough. Escape would not be easy—or clean.

A nineties kid, the New Hire grew up on reruns. Her favorite: syndicated detective stories. *The Rockford Files*, *Miami Vice*, *Moonlighting*. Coming home from school, her babysitters were *Remington Steele*, *Magnum PI*, *Simon & Simon*, and *Hunter*. Like her fictional role models, she would never be content without answers. What would Laura Holt do? Maddie Hayes? Dee Dee McCall?

She needed access to more information. Much of what she knew, or thought she knew, did not make sense. Like slightly expired milk in your coffee, something was off. It wasn't like the hot beverage was wholly undrinkable, but it didn't quite taste right. Or smell right, for that matter.

Starting a full-blown investigation was her calling. The New Hire decided to do what many of her favorite TV counterparts would do: create a murder board. She turned to the back of her notebook and sketched out her initial thoughts. Visually, she had to see how all the players connected. She would gather as much evidence as she could, put together a working hypothesis, and then try to prove it.

Studying her newly drawn diagram, the New Hire thought to look sideways instead of up. What were the connections between the Tech Czar and the VP? With Happiness? With the Stepdaughter? What was the best way to observe people without them knowing? Where they unconsciously, or maybe even subconsciously, revealing all sorts of intimate details? Social Media.

Free to use on the surface, Social Media came with a steep, often hidden, price. While avid users willingly disclose minute details of their lives, seemingly innocuous friends or well-meaning family members often betrayed more casual participants. Knowing the cast of characters she was investigating, the New Hire was confident all of their profiles would be public. They were.

Taking shelter in the green wardrobe room, where she had initially met the VP and Tech Czar, the New Hire began with a popular photo-sharing site. Reviewing the Tech Czar's posts, she scrolled through endless food, sunset, and dog pictures. The New Hire kept an eye on the comment section. It was time-consuming and painful to read through the mindless banter of instant-messaging slang, not to mention the horrific emojis, but she felt it could uncover a not-so-obvious friendship. She appreciated the VP had an alliance with the Tech Czar, but how were Happiness and the Stepdaughter connected? If at all.

The New Hire had assumed Happiness and the Stepdaughter knew each other pre-Startup, but maybe that wasn't true. As she continued to scan yet another photo of Monster, something caught her eye. A picture of Monster and Happiness captioned: "Sunday brunch at the beach. Bottomless mimosas...."

Ugh. Piqued by this discovery, the New Hire went back to Happiness's profile on an employment-oriented social network.

Under her work experience, there were no surprises. In addition to her role at the Startup, Happiness listed herself as owner for the Talent Consulting Firm she had previously mentioned. Included was a California-based fast-food chain as well as a variety of miscellaneous talent-acquisition roles. Scrolling toward the end of the page, the New Hire stopped at the education section. Happiness attended the same university as the Tech Czar. And, yes, at the same time. Under volunteer work, they both listed the same alumni foundation.

The New Hire was disappointed. Choosing to share cocktails with a coworker on a weekend probably indicated a deeper friendship. She wondered if the Chief Happiness Officer's prior relationship influenced her actions, or inactions, at work. Could this explain the Tech Czar's nine lives? It did not mean necessarily that Happiness understood how duplicitous the Tech Czar was, but it could explain how she survived a blatant, and pretty egregious, ethics violation.

The New Hire reflected on some of the conversations she and Happiness shared over the reams of Xerox paper at their desks. Divorced, she was raising two children in a newly renovated Victorian home in a transitional part of town. More than once, Happiness mentioned her contractor. "I'm so frustrated! I'm paying that man thousands to put in a swimming pool. Couldn't he even bother to show up on time?"

She also drove a pricey Range Rover, which seemed a bit extravagant for someone with a single income. The kids had flown to South Carolina to visit their dad, and some of Happiness's commentary surrounding that circumstance led the New Hire to believe he was not particularly well-to-do.

"The kids will be with their loser dad for the holidays this year. They spend the entire week at their grandmother's house. She does all the cooking and all the cleaning. I secretly love when they go, though. When they come home, it's a whole week without complaining."

Other office talk filled the New Hire's head. Happiness had not only several monetary obligations but also expensive tastes.

She and the Stepdaughter often commented on her extensive wardrobe. "Okay, that's definitely a new outfit!" the Stepdaughter would proclaim as she made her way to her desk.

"You guys have seen this before. It's not new," Happiness would reply.

"Um, we definitely have not seen that before. It is absolutely new, and I will forever maintain you own three hundred sixty-five different and unique outfits. Furthermore, we'll never see a repeat set of clothes, because you wouldn't be caught dead wearing the same thing twice!" the New Hire commented.

Happiness was an impeccable dresser, usually in stilettos and Tiffany-branded jewelry. She stood out among the jeans and athleisure wear the rest of the staff wore.

Conscious not to be away from her desk for too long, the New Hire walked back at just the beginning of her investigation. When she sat down, the Stepdaughter was sitting in front of her monitor with several textbooks open.

The New Hire's head was swimming with what she had just discovered. Her trance was interrupted when she heard the Stepdaughter talking.

"Oh hey, I meant to ask you, did it go well at the new gym I recommended?"

"It did! So much better. It even looked somewhat clean. Thanks again for the tip," the New Hire replied. The Stepdaughter had suggested trying an alternate location instead of defaulting to the one closest to the office.

"I can't believe you were going to that scary one! I know it was convenient but too unpredictable. It might appear passable if you're just taking a class or two, but looks can be deceiving. That bathroom. Ooof. My only thought is the bus terminal. Plus, I didn't like you walking there after work."

"True, although you know I'm in-and-out of there within an hour."

"Right, but still, it's dark outside by the time you leave, is it not? I don't think that's too safe. Mine's a way better option."

"Agreed."

The New Hire felt protective of the Stepdaughter. She had, after all, come to her defense when the Tech Czar accused the New Hire of "being a real detective." She empathized with the Stepdaughter's predicament. Due to her relationship with the Founder, and all its connotations, the staff assumed she had secret knowledge. Somehow, she kept hidden when he was going to make a crucial decision or pay everyone's salaries. The Stepdaughter was presumed guilty.

Despite being a natural target of the team's ire, the Stepdaughter stayed above the fray. Insisting she knew nothing of the Founder's dealings, the Stepdaughter would often confide in the New Hire. "Everyone thinks I have some insider knowledge. I don't. I am just working here while I finish my PhD. Trust me, I haven't been paid, either. When I say that, though, no one believes me, so I stay out of it."

"I agree. It's best to stay out of it. I bet it's frustrating. It's not like you are *My Father's Keeper,* or in this case, *Stepfather.*"

"Ha ha. Right! It's not like I grew up with him. I was in high school when he married my mom. When he told me he wanted to start this thing, I wasn't that interested. He was very persistent, though, and insisted it was an opportunity to still work full-time but have the flexibility to take classes. Honestly, that's all I really care about. I had no idea he would get into all these money issues. And that his problems would become my problems!"

Other people at the Startup were not so generous.

"How can you trust her? I think we should ask her where our money is," the Lead Designer complained.

"C'mon, that's not fair. She's in the exact same situation as we are. She isn't getting paid either," the New Hire rebutted, not quite sure if she was convincing her colleague or herself.

"I guess."

"Well, listen, she's still showing up every day. In my mind, if she's coming in, it means we'll be paid, eventually."

"Maybe."

"I know. And remember, I said eventually, meaning not now. Or anytime soon."

Where were her alliances? As much as the New Hire personally liked the Stepdaughter, the Founder was married to her mother. She would often roll her eyes at him and privately disagree with some of his decisions. Plus, she would ignore any directives she did not like. Still, when no other person in the office was able to reach the Founder, the Stepdaughter seemed to have a direct line.

In her early thirties, she had held decent jobs throughout her career, but the Stepdaughter was focused on earning her PhD in Food Science now. She lived in an expensive loft not far from the offices with her boyfriend and his young son. The boyfriend worked in Sales but did not earn enough income to support their lifestyle. The Stepdaughter drove a brand-new Cadillac Escalade with tinted windows and all the upgrades. Her private graduate school had a program fee of more than one hundred thousand.

While Social Media was a good first step for her investigation, the New Hire's mission was now to fill in the gaps. She needed internal documentation. Grabbing her notebook and laptop, she headed over to the green wardrobe room. The shared drive became a treasure trove of information. She found receipts, contracts, nondisclosure agreements, expenses, emergency contacts. The gift that kept on giving. It was like having access to a secret money tree if the tree only produced pennies. One day it could add up to something meaningful, but for now, it was just cents on the dollar.

The results of her initial Social Media search showed a connection between Happiness and the Tech Czar. But how did this connect back to the Founder? Older, he did not have an online presence. All the New Hire's general searches on him came back blank. Almost suspiciously so. Could he have been actively erasing his digital footprint? If so, why was he that deliberate in not leaving an electronic trail?

Another thing about the Startup that did not match its persona was the frequent use of the Xerox machine. At the Search Engine, the New Hire printed so infrequently she still remembered each occasion, and none were work-related. She recalled the two times she flew a low-cost airline (instantly regretting her minimal cost savings) and once for a concert. Printing had evolved out of the New Hire's universe; she had moved fully to digital.

Evidently, not everyone agreed, as a paper-first revivalism was alive-and-well at the Startup. A throwback to an earlier era when trees were considered an unlimited resource. Thinking about the prominence the printer served in the lives of the employees, the New Hire wondered what secrets the machine kept.

Part of the New Hire's company training included an extensive process on filing expenses. Most of it was straightforward. Fill out the template itemizing all expenditures, scan the corresponding physical receipts, and email it to the Office Manager. After sending electronically, employees were to print out their reports and submit them to Happiness. Since the Office Manager processed the requests, the New Hire saw no reason to then print a copy for Happiness to file. Why not just track digitally? She always skipped the last step.

The New Hire realized each time someone in the office printed a file, the machine logged a temporary record. In case of a paper jam, a toner error, or a lack of ink, the job would remain in the memory until it was full. Anyone could go to the printer's setting, look at the log, and reprint the document directly from the machine.

Perhaps something interesting could be found?

The printer had a natural advantage: Organically, it lived in an out-of-the-way place to avoid interrupting employees with its constant noise. Most of the staff in the office seemed occupied by one thing or another, so the New Hire made her way over to the machine. Casually looking around, she hit a few buttons on the touchpad. Selecting the main menu, she easily found the log and observed a few choice selections:

prototype 0315

AMEX0628471

one-pet-to-live_may

dr harris invoice

investor deck final

investor deck final final

new investor deck final

my receipts_apr

my receipts_may

A few looked promising, but **AMEX** was a top contender. To minimize her trips to the printer, the New Hire reprinted **AMEX0628471**, **my receipts_apr**, and **my receipts_may.** Standing over the machine, she watched anxiously as the warm papers stacked up. She grabbed each sheet individually and, once complete, walked back to her desk.

Perusing the papers at her seat, the New Hire was surprised **my receipts_apr** and **my receipts_may** resulted in little insight. The printouts were a random collection of restaurants and a gym membership invoice. Nothing worth following up. The last document, **AMEX0628471**, was the motherlode.

What the New Hire uncovered was the Founder's monthly American Express Platinum card statement for May. Glad she was already sitting down, the New Hire's jaw must have surely looked like it hit the floor. He made the previous month's payment of one hundred and ten thousand dollars. The charges for the current month: eighty-eight thousand dollars. Money was a problem, but apparently only for the Startup employees hoping to get paid regularly.

Going line by line, the New Hire noticed inconsistencies. Personal and business expenses intermingled. There were airline tickets to Europe for the Founder's recently graduated daughter. A big expense from a high-end jewelry store. Multiple charges at reservations-months-in-advance restaurants.

Something else stood out: the Shared Workspace Solutions Company owned the account.

The New Hire felt she was beginning to make inroads. Nothing definitive, but she recognized she was entering a path that might not lead to a happy conclusion. If she continued, the road ahead might be bumpy. Worse, she thought, more unanswered questions. Fasten your seatbelt.

Next to her monitor staring at her sat the set of keys given to her by the Office Manager. Three, to be exact. One unlocked the visitor's entrance to enter through the front area. Another opened the theater. The third key was unknown. The Office Manager told her it opened everything else, but what did that mean? Since it was the same shape and size as the others, it must be for another locked door in the large open-plan space. *But where were the other locked doors?*

Since the New Hire knew the office layout well, the door must not be somewhere obvious. Somewhere out of sight. In her head, she created a mental map. The only area she had never really explored was the back office. There were the two wardrobe rooms there, but what else? The IT room? The spot where the Senior Technology Specialist conducted obviously urgent business, as he was always interrupting confidential meetings with the Founder.

The New Hire checked her phone for the time. It was approaching lunch, the roughly two-hour period where most of the staff would be gone. It was Taco Tuesday. The Tech team would be leaving soon. Fairly confident enough staff would clear out shortly, the New Hire planned her clandestine operation.

Her head was swimming. She kept one eye on the time displayed in the upper corner of her computer screen. Distracted, the New Hire was startled when Happiness said, "Hey, aren't you joining us for lunch?"

"Oh. Um, you know what, you guys should go without me today."

"What? No, just come. We'll make it quick."

"I know. It's not like I don't want to go, but I should stay. I'm right in the middle of something. I just want to finish it, you know? What if I promise to go with y'all tomorrow?"

"Are you sure? We can wait for you?"

"Nah, it's fine. Thank you. If I get it done early, I can meet you, okay? Pirate Bar, right?"

"Ha ha! Of course! Yeah, come if you can. Text if you want us to bring you something back."

"I will. I will. Don't have fun without me."

"No promises."

With Happiness and the Stepdaughter heading out to lunch and the Tech team already gone, the New Hire felt confident to explore. She looked around. A few of the Investigative Reporters were at their desks, but as usual, they were consumed with themselves. Most looked to be browsing the web. It was unclear if it was personal or professional research.

"Did you see over the weekend was the last-ever circus?" the Editor said.

"The last ever?" the Investigative Reporter replied.

"Well, for Ringling Brothers and Barnum and Bailey, anyway."

"Ah. That's sad. I mean, it's sad, but, like, not sad, right? Aren't we supposed to hate circuses now?"

"Yeah, totally. Circuses are bad. Boo circuses!"

"Sad about Ringling Bros, though."

"Yeah."

The New Hire grabbed her phone and headed toward the back office. Past the wardrobe area, she saw the IT server room. Taking the key from her pocket, she inserted it into the hole. It fit. She turned the knob and opened the door.

The IT server room revealed an excess of computer equipment and supplies. MacBook Pros. Monitors. Wireless keyboards and mice. The room was surprisingly neat. Organized chaos. The New Hire imagined this was Eavesdropping Central. The headquarters for reading all emails, listening in on all phone calls, and secretly recording the meeting rooms.

In addition to the plethora of supplies, the New Hire noticed a half-empty soda can, a crumbled potato chip bag, and high-end headphones. Looking carefully at the headphones, she was sure she had finally uncovered proof of Senior Technology Specialist's misdeeds. Like her favorite TV detectives on a stakeout, the New Hire imagined the other end of the wire led to an old-fashioned recording device. As her eyes followed the cable, she saw it plugged into an extra laptop.

Senior Technology used the room to stream movies.

Of course he did.

CHAPTER 10

REFLECTIONS

Office space exploration was a bust. Feeling she had hit a dead end, the New Hire did not know where to focus next. She needed a clue. A puzzle piece. A way forward. What she had learned so far was "there was always money in the banana stand." The Shared Workspace Solutions Company owned the credit card funding the Startup. The Founder had huge overhead and commingled personal and business expenses. Back to the drawing board. She had a few dots but nothing to connect them together.

After a longer-than-usual wage drought, the New Hire received a long-overdue paycheck. Scanning to see if the amount included a bonus, she noticed something else. Something she had overlooked many times before: an address.

The once-prominent department store's former headquarters, where for nearly ten months the New Hire had shown up daily, was not listed on her paystub. How could something so simple, so omnipresent, so seemingly innocuous, be hidden in plain sight right from the beginning?

However, the listed street name and the suite number were instantly recognizable. It housed the wholly separate Shared Workspace Solutions Company, where the Founder spent most of his working hours. While not entirely sure of the full implications, combined with the credit card statement, it was becoming more probable that the Startup was secretly owned by the Shared Workspace Solutions Company. Best-case scenario: light fraud. Worst-case: money laundering.

Each day, the New Hire collected more evidence. She created a personal database of important information, intentionally saving it on a thumb drive. Undeterred in her mission to unlock the Startup's secrets, the New Hire spent her days balancing her core responsibilities with her detective work.

The Mobile App development was moving forward. She ensured crucial tasks were completed quickly to avoid unwanted scrutiny. Equally as methodical, she was carving out private sessions to pour through documents on the shared server. It was not like she was going to find a folder labeled: **Do Not Read**. This operation was going to take time.

While the Tech Czar often spoke of the importance of cybersecurity, the New Hire was confident she took shortcuts. Careless data storage would not be unique to the Startup. When the New Hire worked at the Search Engine, she remembered when a Senior Director accidentally uploaded the entire staff's individual ranking (and yes, everyone on the team was assigned a numerical value from one to fifty) and salary to a shared drive. From that day forth, the New Hire always password-protected any files with confidential data. She was positive no one else in the company did.

Each day, the New Hire would make a little progress yet no progress at all. She kept pushing. And worrying. The New Hire not only worried about getting caught investigating the company she worked for but also if she was culpable.

If the Startup was committing fraud, was she compliant? Complicit? Was she any better than her peers? She liked getting paid her somewhat inflated salary. She enjoyed the unearned cash bonuses (until they stopped). She even secretly enjoyed the lack of personal responsibility and individual goals that had weighed on her so heavily in previous roles.

The New Hire grew particularly nostalgic for jobs past. Memories in the corner of her mind, she wanted them misty and watercolored.

Looking back (What a funny concept. *Shouldn't we always be looking forward?*), she felt stuck. Trapped. The ship was sinking, but it was unclear where the leak was coming from. Plus, even if she could stop the rush of water threatening her survival, what was her end game?

The Startup had an incredibly loose structure, but technically, Design reported to her. She felt a sense of obligation. What could she say? The New Hire did not have any direct proof of specific wrongdoing. As a manager, the New Hire also had an obligation to the company. As a human, she had an obligation to her coworkers. At any job, people get paid a mutually agreed-upon sum to follow directions. It does not matter what is in an individual title. A portion of every person's salary is to take a deep breath, close his or her eyes, and look the other way.

To the New Hire, fraud made sense. The fake construction. The placeholder website. The missing Mobile App. Why was the Founder so determined to push this project out, though? What was he trying to accomplish? If it was simple fraud, why go through all the pretense? The hiring. The firing. The drama.

The Founder had a different mindset. Maybe the rest of the Executive staff did too. The New Hire believed in the Social Contract. Unwritten Rules. Decency. For the most part, people adhered to these guiding principles. Over time, however—and especially in the business world—the New Hire realized she was the only fool playing by those rules.

The Founder had a way of owning everything. Ironically, things were not paid with legal tender, but rather with one's devotion. The perfect antidote for the times. Here was the answer. Here was the solution. No thinking necessary. Someone to believe in. Someone to follow. Only the Founder could provide hope. Only the Founder could provide a livelihood. Only the Founder could show the way.

Beneath the mask, however, there wasn't any depth. No substance. Just a wizard controlled by a small man behind his emerald-green curtain. The Founder did not have certitude. He did not have a vision. His views could change instantly, depending, of course, on whoever spoke to him last.

His enablers figured out how to persuade him without telling him what to do. They would plant the seeds, flame the fires, and leave the embers slowly burning. The discarded ashes did not have to be stoked. It was enough to let them simmer. Eventually, the Founder's own doubt would circulate in his head, creating the needed oxygen and fuel necessary to reignite the fire, always teetering on the verge of flameout.

The Founder knew he was building a house of cards. His exterior looked impeccable. So shiny and bright. Golden. The team would construct their own futures in his glow. Exaggerating his thoughts, his impact. Giving greater importance to his words over their expertise and experience, or more likely, their lack of expertise and experience.

Most of the Executive team was under his spell. Without their compliance and complicity, the engine would not run. They still could throw the occasional wrench, but the truth was the Executive team needed the Founder more than he needed them. He fulfilled a critical function of telling them what they wanted to hear.

The New Hire wondered what is it was like to have no consequences. How could people not be responsible for their transgressions? She could not relate. Cause and effect weighed heavily on her conscience. Even if there were any repercussions, did this breed of people care? Were they all just playing by different rules? Unwritten ones that seem to ebb and flow as necessary to warrant any action taken by the Founder. Did they figure out some greater truth that the New Hire failed to see, or couldn't see, due to her sense of justice? Her idea of right or wrong?

The Founder was playing a zero-sum game. The end always justifies the means. Whatever move made had no effect. His script adapted immediately, accounting for all conceivable scenarios. If someone said up, he said down. If someone said down, he said up. Whatever option, his response was presented with such conviction. Ordained from above, he was on the righteous path.

Along the way, the Founder picked up accomplices—some knowing and maybe some unaware. Once they entered the inner sanctum, what happened? The New Hire was in the inner sanctum. Were only the willing ones initiated into the club? What did the Tech Czar, the VP, Happiness, and even the Stepdaughter all have in common? The New Hire wanted to think the Stepdaughter was different, but maybe not.

The Founder was powerful, always in control. A provider. He was a decision-maker but overwhelmed, desperate for the next big deal. Each time the New Hire saw the Founder, she knew he had aged. Not a lot, but just enough. He needed all the cards in his elaborate house of cards to stay in place. Against time. Against nature. Against common sense. One more day, one more score. The Founder was borrowing from Peter to pay Paul next week.

In one way or another, the Tech Czar, the VP, Happiness, and even the Stepdaughter needed money. All had different reasons and levels of desperation.

The Stepdaughter grew up in privilege with her mother and her mother's husband, the Founder. Her mother had struggled financially until the second marriage. The union brought not only wealth but also a plethora of half-siblings, ranging from twenty years older to ten years younger. The Stepdaughter had biological siblings too, making for a true modern family.

She was a realist. She saw people for who and what they were. She had a way of not letting it interfere with her plans. She was ambitious and had definitive goals: Stay at the Startup while earning her PhD. Something easy but high-paying. A transitional job. Was the Founder paying for the Stepdaughter's tuition? Her three-bedroom loft apartment in a luxury skyscraper? Her brand-new SUV? The New Hire knew she was collecting a biweekly salary but wondered what else.

She knew how to have fun, but it came with a price tag. She was used to a certain lifestyle. "I went to that new bar in Los Feliz last night with my roommates from college. It was, like, the first night out I had in forever. My boyfriend took his son to his mom's, so I didn't even feel guilty," the Stepdaughter said.

"Highlights? Lowlights?" the New Hire inquired.

"No lowlights. It was just nice catching up with those girls. And we all agreed to rent a house again this year for Coachella. It's super expensive, but whatever. To avoid the shuttle, you have to book something within walking distance of the venue. And, I mean, if you're gonna be within walking distance, you need the VIP tickets. Yeah, like I said, not cheap, but it'll be great."

"So fun. I love it."

"Oh, you know, living my best life."

"You do, don't you?"

The Stepdaughter would describe herself as authentic. The New Hire genuinely liked her directness, realness, and overall laid-back style. Perhaps what the New Hire admired most was how the Stepdaughter observed everything without being noticed. She would take note and save it for either a rainy day or when it might serve some purpose.

On the other side of the spectrum, the Tech Czar was way over her head. As best as the New Hire could piece together, she had levered her alumni connections to land the job. It must have been so easy for the Tech Czar to make promises of things she knew little about to someone like the Founder, so eager for the quick win. Someone to slot in. An instant match. Her talk about big ideas would have appealed to him. What he could not have known was once it came time to implement something, anything, the Tech Czar was out of her depth.

Well-off, she habitually spoke about her beachfront house. Her condo in Las Vegas. Rental properties throughout the state. She frequently complained about her operating costs. The Tech Czar was supporting an ex-wife, who she dumped for a newer model. With the new wife came a stepchild, the kid. Like the Founder, she needed the money to be constantly flowing. She created several opportunities, including unethical ones, to do that.

Happiness earned a great salary but was completely over-extended too. She had recently bought an investment property, so was cash-poor. Unlike most people who invest for their future, Happiness was not willing to make the sacrifices to live on a budget. Like the Founder, she was living paycheck to paycheck. She was terrified of not having money to support her extravagant lifestyle.

Even though Happiness had a family of three, her house had eight bedrooms. Over the lunch table, she would often show the New Hire pictures of the latest renovation project. She wanted to extend the kitchen and dining room into a single space. Due to Happiness's expensive tastes, the New Hire was taken aback by the country-chic decor; she had pegged her way more modern. From the photos, the house looked great when you first entered. Like a story book. Upstairs, however, half the rooms were empty.

The VP had been raised in a prominent and somewhat important family in Los Angeles. She mentioned familial pressures. "My father was the County Chair for several years," often interjected with a casualness.

Supremely proud, it quietly killed her when her husband lost his job. "Yes, I am the breadwinner now!" was a recurrent complaint, dripping with disbelief and a clumsy attempt to reframe the situation in a more positive light.

The New Hire continued her research, browsing more carefully to see what she could have missed from her initial investigation. Knowing there was a definite connection between the Founder's two businesses, she visited the Shared Workspace Solutions Company's website again.

The webpages, built from a template, looked straightforward with a subsection describing Our Mission, Our Services, Testimonials, and a Contact page. The address and phone number matched her paycheck.

The New Hire scanned the company bios. She expected to find the Founder, front and center. He was suspiciously missing. Neither his name nor his picture appeared anywhere on the page. Something else was askew.

Reviewing the names and faces of the Shared Workspace Solutions Company employees, the New Hire noted one man stood out. He was significantly younger than the other professionals pictured. Also, he had two first names. The type of double names that seemed like they should be hyphenated rather than designating a distinctive first and wholly separate last name. Like a Jimmy John, Billy Bob, or Richie Rich.

Even more unusual, though, the man pictured was a dead ringer for the Founder.

CHAPTER 11

WISE UP

Life isn't like the movies. It is filled with unknowns. There is no smoking gun. No definitive sign. No single piece of evidence proves your suspicions beyond a reasonable doubt. Usually, it is an impression. Maybe a faint one. Just an instinct. Something doesn't feel right. Doesn't look right. Doesn't sound right.

For the New Hire, she could see her options slowly fading away. Survival was questionable. This wasn't like the usual scraps and squabbles she could usually outmaneuver eventually. This was different. Quicksand.

For someone who prided herself on being able to think herself out of most situation, ideas failed her. It was time to start digging, and fast. While the New Hire wanted to turn to her newly acquired friends, she knew better. Too bad; she really liked them.

All the warning signs were there, looking back. In fact, she could practically hear them read out like a prosecutor's opening brief:

Did you or did you not have minimal assignments? Incompetent coworkers? Inconsistent pay?

You said construction always seemed to be in progress, correct? Didn't you also state you never saw a single construction worker? Never?

Do you think it is commonplace for a workplace, one you claimed that provided free food, to take away its water cooler? What happened to the water?

None of this struck you as unusual for an alleged place of business?

Your honor, I submit to the court, the defendant realized all along what was happening and was a willing participant in this clear and present deception!

Finding what appeared to be a dead ringer for the Founder on the Shared Workspace Solutions Company's website meant something, but the New Hire was not sure what. Where could she go to learn more about this man? Where do people self-identify themselves, plus categorize others they know? It was time to revisit Social Media.

Using the name listed on the Shared Workplace Solutions Company's site, the New Hire's search began. The man pictured looked slightly older than the Stepdaughter, so definitely a child from the Founder's first marriage. Within seconds, an online profile popped up, visually matching the photo she observed earlier. The First Son had tagged his siblings and mother in several photos. *Yes, Virginia, we have a match.*

What did this prove? Nepotism was alive and well? Why did the First Son conceal his identity on the Shared Workspace Solutions website, using two such obvious first names? A clear attempt to mask a familial connection, but why? The Founder's name did not appear anywhere on the site.

Feeling as though the Shared Workplace Solutions Company was likely more than just a day job for the Founder, the New Hire was driven to find the truth. She had a compulsion. She wanted to understand how the companies connected beyond the obvious. This was a way of life. A family business. An enterprise.

The New Hire needed to investigate the construction site again. Maybe there was some paperwork carelessly left behind or an unintentional detail on an otherwise benign document. Finding the right time to explore, she made her way down to the sixth floor.

Hyperaware of her surroundings, the New Hire ensured she was alone. She could hear every paranoid person's personal anthem in her head, Rockwell's one-hit-wonder.

Intentionally, she walked past the construction site before doubling back to the unlocked door. More than six months had passed since her first foray into the construction zone, but once again, it looked like the place where time stood still. Abandoned. Empty. A ghost town. Her second search did not turn up anything.

Retracing her steps, the New Hire was ready to leave. As she carefully pulled the door shut, she read the legally required posted notification on the entrance. She paid close attention to the listed construction company name. She took a photo of the printed paper copy. She had hoped the address matched that of the Founder's Shared Workspace Solutions Company. It did not.

Slightly defeated, the New Hire went back to her online research. She must have missed something.

Feeling more anxious, as if her coworkers were mentally keeping track of her whereabouts, the New Hire took more precautions. Returning to her desk from an extended absence, she made a point of checking in with Happiness and the Stepdaughter. She wanted to keep up appearances. She also felt the need to create a little coverage.

"Hey, did you guys see there is a new cereal bar around the block?"

"A cereal bar? I am intrigued. What is that?" asked the Stepdaughter.

"Well, as the name implies, it's an entire café-bar filled only with outrageously sweet cereals and disgustingly flavored milk. We have to go."

"Hmm. I am not convinced," Happiness chimed in.

"What? We have to go. I mean, at least once. How bad could it be? It's cereal."

"Fun! I am totally in. C'mon, it'll be different. We should go," the Stepdaughter urged a reluctant Happiness.

"Okay, fine. But if I do not like my cereal, you are paying," Happiness said.

"Fine. I think my money's safe. They are only open in the mornings, though, so we should pick a day. I will send you guys an invitation for next Friday?"

The New Hire felt conflicted. While eager to deflect self-imagined suspicions from her friends, she really did enjoy spending time with them. She just wasn't sure she knew who they really were. Plus, the New Hire really did want to try that cereal bar.

Recharged, the New Hire walked to the kitchen. Someone brought some coffee capsules from home, so she grabbed a fresh cup of joe and continued her mission. She would live to fight another day.

* * *

While planning her next move, the New Hire recognized she needed a more methodical approach. More systematic. For the next phase of the investigation, she also required more privacy. This type of recon was not possible at her desk. After checking her surroundings, the New Hire headed back to the wardrobe rooms, still conscious of every minute away from her desk.

She returned to the shared drive for a more thorough exploration. The folder headings were self-explanatory. Product, Design, and IT. The New Hire expanded the folders' names to take a deeper dive. She clicked on a few files, finding nothing out of the ordinary. PowerPoint decks, images, and prototypes.

Since the wardrobe room did not have any windows, every noise was exaggerated. The extraordinary bright lights were beating down on her face. She imagined herself back at her initial interview. An interrogation was her initial thought on that day. Now, she was the inquisitor. As the New Hire continued reading file names, she stopped on a folder named Admin. If there was anything to be found, it would be there.

Investigating with fresh eyes, the New Hire saw several subfolders. Contact Sheet, Office Equipment, Expenses, Operating Procedures, Templates. Her eyes fixed on Expenses. Each month, she had been documenting her work-related costs and submitting them to be reimbursed. She had memorized the meticulous, overly detailed process from her first week at the Startup.

On edge, she continued down the rabbit hole, digging deeper into the Expenses folder. Organized by month, the New Hire noticed a rollup report of what everyone had expensed. She clicked around. What she expected: gym reimbursements, lunch receipts, and office equipment invoices. No surprises.

From her previous experience at the Search Engine, at least once a quarter, some executive would leave his expenses on the Xerox machine. Inevitably, the most easily outraged person in the office would see this accidentally left behind confidential report and complain. "Two thousand dollars for a client lunch! How's that plausible? That's more than my rent! Guess what the total amount for the month is? I hope you are sitting down, because that dope is expensing twenty-five grand a month! A month!"

The New Hire inspected the remaining file names in the Expenses folder, looking for anything out of place. Dates and last names. Then, she came across something interesting: **archive1**.

What could that be?

As the New Hire opened the file, a familiar umbrella logo caught her eye. She found the Startup's most recent monthly statement from the business bank account. Knowing she had something important, the New Hire downloaded a copy to her thumb drive and emailed herself from a personal web-based account. She exited out of the server and viewed her offline copy.

Jackpot.

The New Hire slowly opened the door to the wardrobe room to check if the coast was clear. She stood in the doorway for a minute. She heard a noise. A knot formed in her stomach.

She took another step forward and saw a flash go by. Shaken to her core, she realized it must be a mouse, no doubt enjoying the playground of carelessly left food and millions of crumbs everywhere. Slightly terrified that a mouse was nearby but relieved no humans were, the New Hire returned to the green wardrobe room. She sat back down tentatively, careful to keep her feet off the floor, just in case.

In the file, the New Hire scanned the bill for something to process. Her eyes stopped on the Checking Activity Summary.

Beginning balance: $294.27.

Ending balance: $1,625.59.

No wonder she had stopped getting paid regularly.

As the New Hire read further, she went through the descriptions of the daily activities. One column listed debits, another credits, and a final stated the balance.

The New Hire went line-by-line, using her finger to guide her glance. Office expenditures, personal expenses, and salaries all in one place. Wire transfers in. Wire transfers out. Two hundred thousand dollars from the Founder's Shared Workspace Solutions Company in. Money, obviously, not well-spent, considering the final balance.

Throughout the month, huge sums of money went back-and-forth from the Shared Workspace Solutions Company and the Startup through these wire transfers. The Shared Workspace Solutions Company's name was not listed as the recipient, but the New Hire immediately recognized the corporate address.

The New Hire pulled out her phone. She scrolled through her camera roll for the photo she had taken at the construction site.

Match.

Another recipient of a substantial dollar amount. She recognized another company name. It was Happiness's Talent Consulting Firm. The one she had nonchalantly mentioned to the New Hire.

The Chief Happiness Officer was not only clearing a hefty salary from the Startup, but also charging consulting fees of twenty thousand. In all probability, the Founder didn't realize Happiness owned the Talent Consulting Firm and that he was paying her twice. Like the Tech Czar, she was self-dealing. Except successfully.

Then, there it was. Like picking up a rock and seeing everything underneath you don't want to see. A balloon payment. Forty thousand dollars. Forty. Thousand. Dollars.

The recipient? The Stepdaughter. The New Hire felt sick.

She could not be stopped now. The New Hire continued pouring over the data, expecting to see additional payments to the Tech Czar. She didn't. She expected to see additional payments to the VP. She didn't.

The New Hire felt the pressure building in the corner of her right eye, forcing her to press the bridge of her nose as if she was wearing a pair of glasses that had been worn for too long.

The VP had to work. Her husband had been out of work for more than a year. She reeked of desperation, and the Founder knew it. Even though the VP was earning an obscenely inflated salary, she was not taking additional funds. She chose to be an awful person. Surprisingly, the Tech Czar, who was flat-out unethical and tried to scam the company by outsourcing to herself, was also not on the take.

The two people to whom the New Hire felt a sincere connection, however, were complicit. The bank records proved it while absolving the Tech Czar and the VP. How ironic; they were just horrible people.

Sitting in disbelief, the New Hire was numb. She felt like someone had plunged a knife, edgy and dull, into her soul. She felt betrayed. In their time working together, she had felt a genuine closeness with the Stepdaughter and Happiness. Maybe they would not be taking weekend trips to the Grand

Tetons together, but they were colleagues. Chums. She liked them. She enjoyed their lunches together. She trusted them. They had been her camp friends for the entire summer and then some.

Over and over and over again, the Stepdaughter had denied having any involvement in the Founder's wrongdoings. "He is married to my mom," had been a frequent refrain suggesting a certain amount of detachment. Her deception felt deeper. More intense. More painful. Blood on the tracks.

The New Hire walked back to her desk from the wardrobe room, taking in her surroundings in a different way, a more critical view. She saw wires everywhere. Modems placed in the corner of the ceiling with bright blue LAN cords streaming down. As she walked past the kitchen, she thought how it never seemed clean. The forest-green plastic covering had a furniture polish sparkle, but the rust-stained sink had long ago lost its shine.

She noticed the jumble of wires in the middle of each bank of desks. Power outlets loaded with plugs for monitors, laptops, and cell phones. The New Hire scanned the office, still clutching the thumb drive in her left hand.

She observed the VP standing over the Lead Designer, the one she once tried to get fired. "I need to approve any plans to move forward. I'm not sure if I'm happy with these layouts."

On the other side, just turning the corner, the New Hire overheard the Tech Czar on her cell phone. "Are you sure Kong is not eating? Did you try adding a little pumpkin to her dry food? Hmm. Okay. Yeah, yeah. Well, maybe you are right, and we should take her to the vet. I can leave the office now."

The Chief Happiness Officer was sitting at her desk shopping for designer purses. She was toggling between two tabs, debating on which look would go better with the stylish pantsuits on her second screen.

Next to Happiness, the New Hire noticed the Stepdaughter's monitor was shut down. All her schoolbooks were missing too, so she must have already left for the day.

The New Hire approached her chair, seeing the people from the News Department hard at work. Investigating the big story as always. Literally missing the even bigger one right in front of their noses.

Par for the course.

Without saying a word, she disconnected the laptop charger, slowly wrapping the cord and placing it into her shoulder bag. She felt the weight of the thumb drive still in her hand. She examined her desk for what remained. A pen, a notebook, and her well-traveled statue of the Queen, a gift from former coworkers on the day she became a British citizen. Solar-powered, the Queen's wrist perpetually glided back-and-forth. The Royal Wave.

Next to the monitor, her free promotional mug read: *Unbreakable Kimmy Schmidt.* The New Hire smiled. The cup had an inch of black coffee from earlier in the day. She caught the eye of one of the Investigative Reporters.

"Hey, I think someone on your team dropped this. I found it on the floor earlier," the New Hire said, handing over the thumb drive with the incriminating bank records.

"Oh, okay. Thank you."

"Yep."

As the New Hire grabbed her purse, she looked around, knowing she would never return.

ACKNOWLEDGMENTS

I would like acknowledge the family and friends who have encouraged me with love, kindness, and support, not only through this entire process, but always:

AJ S., Alec M., Alessandra B., Allison P., Allyson B., Alyson M., Amana V., Americ N., Andrew K., Andrew T., Brandon M., Brenda S., Bryan S., Cadi J., Charles B., Chris B., Christa M., Cindy P., Conor B., Dan K., Danielle M., Danny M., Dave M., Dave P., David S., Debbie T., Debbie Y., Diana M., Diana R., Dragos P., Ed D., Eileen M., Emily S., Evans B., Frank P., Gaetano C., Gail M., George F., Gerald D., Gerard S., Gerry E., Gurpreet P., Henrique M., Herb M., Hillary Z., Immy B., Jackie P., Jackson M., Jaimie M., James B., Jameson M., Janine H., Jason T., Jeff J., Jeff M., Jen S., Jenna C., Jenny A., Jenny C., Jerry B., Jess M., Jesse I., Jim O., Joe M., Joe V., John M., John P., Jonathan H., Jonathan W., Josh D., Josh L., Justin S., Karen I., Kari H., Kate H., Kelly F., Kris G., Krishnan J., Kristen S., Kristiana C., Laura M., Lauren F., Laurie K., Leeann N., Leigh K., Linda D., Linda W., Lisa J., Maeve M., Maggie L., Marla M., Marly R., Marsha I., Mary M., Matt K., Matt M., Meron C., Micah M., Michelle C., Mick M., Mike F., Mike M., Mike S., Naoshi Y., Nick B., Owen B., Pam H., Paul H., Petra K., Ralph J., Rebecca M., Rob W., Rob Z., Rocky L.,

Sam B., Sara S., Scott M., Sean M., Sharon S., Shelley C., Sherien K., Shilpa N., Sophie P., Stacey S., Stef R., Stephen C., Steve S., Tiffany E., Tiffany I., Tracy A., Val M., Wendy P., and Yami M.

To my Three's Company crew, you mean more to me than you could possibly know: Jack S., Janet S., and Chrissy S.

If it takes a village, well, I was lucky enough to get an entire city. In countless ways, these folks helped shape the final story—from beginning to middle to end. Thank you. I am forever grateful:

Audra O.	Liza S.
Barbara F	Lorraine M.
Ben O.	Lynda S.
Dena J.	Pamela B.
Doris B.	Rob K.
Jennifer G.	Steve S.

Thank you, New Degree Press. The machine keeps running because of the entire team's dedication and drive. A special call out to Eric K., Lauren M., Kristy C., Brian B., and, of course, Carol M. I appreciate it.

CPSIA information can be obtained
at www.ICGtesting.com
Printed in the USA
FSHW021631251021

9 781636 767093